IOMAS

REFLECTIONS

ON

LIFE

AND

LIVING

First edition 2007
Published in Dublin, Ireland by Jordan Publishers 2007

Copyright © Joanna Jordan 2007

Quotations used under "fair use".

Pen & Ink drawings x 52 Copyright © Joanna Jordan 2007
Cover photograph "Tulip" Copyright © Joanna Jordan 2007

ISBN 978-0-9556457-0-9

Cover design by Marion Cronin

Printed in Ireland by ColourBooks Ltd.

DISCLAMER

The ideas put forward in this book are strictly those of the author. So take what you like and leave the rest.

IOMAS

REFLECTIONS ON LIFE AND

LIVING

JOANNA JORDAN

IOMAS is the Gaelic word for intuition.

It is pronounced "e – o - maus".

A BLESSING

May every person whose hand touches this book or whose ear
hears these words be blessed a thousandfold, they themselves
and every member of their family tree back seven generations
and down to the present day.

JOANNA JORDAN

This book is dedicated to my little ones: Ann, Beatrice, Margaret, Sarah Rachel, Mary and Michael, Deirdre and finally Dermot.

IOMAS

REFLECTIONS ON LIFE AND

LIVING

JOANNA JORDAN

CONTENTS

                                                      PAGE
Weekly Quotations…Starting Week 1……….. 1.

Daily Reflections…...Starting Week 1 Day 1… 2.

Weekly Pen & Ink

Drawings……………Starting Week 1 Day 7… 8.

END PAGES

Pen & Ink Drawings …………………………… 417.

Index …………………………………………... 421.

Sources of Daily Quotations…………………… 428.

Additional Sources of Weekly Quotations…….. 431.

"As long as man does not live in the truth, he cannot taste real freedom."

THE FATHER

WEEK 1

"I fill you with My love, then you have only to ask me for the virtues and perfection you need and you can be sure that in those moments when God is reposing in His creatures, nothing will be refused you."

THE FATHER

"The Lord loveth a cheerful receiver, as well as a cheerful giver....If one has been a bad receiver he must become a good one, take even a postage stamp if it is given him, and open up his channels for receiving."

FLORENCE SCOVEL SHINN

I remember once been given a 1p postage stamp and being much offended. At the time I was hoping for more. Now I pick up pennies or cents from the street and say "Thank you, Lord". Once during a time of financial lack, my son reached into his pocket and offered me the few pence that he had. At first I said "No keep it", but then I realised that he was offering me all the money he had in the world, and I accepted it. Money started to come in slowly but steadily and in increasing amounts after that.

Accept everything; every little thing that comes to you is from God, no matter what the appearance. Pennies are signs of pounds, and pounds the signs of hundreds and thousands. Do not set any limits to God's generosity. Accept all, little and large, as a gift and move it on. Do not hoard. Money is to be used, to be spent, to be enjoyed. Use it and more will come to replace it. Keep it moving. Ask for what you need and what ever you want for yourself and others. Ask for it to come in perfect ways and at the perfect time. Ask only for what is yours by divine right.

"Infinite Spirit open the way for great abundance for --------- .
She is an irresistible magnet for all that belongs to her by
divine right."

FLORENCE SCOVEL SHINN

This is an affirmation. In the -------- you put your own
name or the name of the person you wish this for, changing the
pronouns as appropriate. Repeat this to yourself or out loud
many times.

God or the "Infinite Spirit" wishes only the best for us,
wishes all of us to have "great abundance" but we must believe
that we are entitled to it and believe that we deserve it. We
must see ourselves living it and ask for it. We must ask for the
divine selection or what is ours by "divine right". Ask God to
pick the right partner, the right job or the right accommodation
for you or others. When you ask for the divine selection it will
come to you in time and in a perfect way. Let go of wanting a
specific thing or situation. You may get it but with negative
consequences. Always ask for the divine selection, what is
yours by divine right.

"Understanding and action proceeding from understanding and guided by it, is the one weapon against the world's bombardment, the one medicine, the one instrument by which liberty, health, and joy may be shaped or shaped towards, in the individual, and in the race."

                    JAMES AGREE with WALKER EVANS

       Understanding is not just an intellectual understanding. True understanding is a knowing, a clarity of vision, a sudden and clear knowing of what is the right course of action to take, or what is the truth of the situation you are facing.

       This clarity of vision is a gift from God, a totality of mind and body. It is of rightness. It is a deep down feeling about the correctness of a situation or the right course of action you need to take.

       When these moments of clarity come hold on to them, write them down, share them with a trusted friend. Reread them when moments of doubt come, when fear, confusion or rationalizations threaten to take over.

"If all men were to bring their miseries together in one place, most would be glad to take each his own home again rather than take a portion out of the common stock."

SOLON

All the problems, difficulties and challenges that we have to deal with are tailor made for us. They are there for a reason. There is something for us to learn from every situation. If trials press hard it could be that we are going in the wrong direction. We may be in the wrong marriage, the wrong job or the wrong line of traffic. The people we react strongly to could be mirroring our own weakness to us. For example: our own indecision. They could be re-enacting situations from our childhoods with our own mothers and fathers or lack of them. So the question is not why are they the way they are but why am I reacting so strongly to them? In difficult situations the question is not why is this happening to me or what did I do to deserve this but what can I learn from this?

The quicker you learn your lessons the less often they will have to be repeated.

"Take time to be friendly – it is the road to happiness,
Take time to dream – it is hitching your way on to a star.
Take time to love and be loved – it is the privilege of the gods.
Take time to look around – it is too short a day to be selfish.
Take time to laugh – it is the music of the soul."

OLD ENGLISH PRAYER

Time is very precious nowadays. Modern life forces us to spend time in queues, in traffic jams, waiting on the telephone and waiting for or on public transport. All religious and spiritual disciplines recommend daily time out, time for the reading of spiritual matters, time for prayer and time for meditation. So the next time you are sitting on a bus or train you can close your eyes and pray. You can pray for yourself, for all the people you care about and all the people who annoy you or anger you and you can pray for all the people on the bus as well.

"Love and fear cannot dwell together. By their very natures they cannot exist side by side. Evil is powerful and fear is one of evil's most potent forces."

TWO LISTENERS

This is definitely true. Fear is the most destructive force. There is however one kind of fear which is healthy. It is a kind of warning. It says do not do this, do not go there, run away quickly. It is a short sharp warning. It is felt in your gut and with it comes the energy to take action.

Destructive fear paralyses; it freezes. It stops you from doing things. It is not from God and it is not good. Ask yourself why am I doing this? If your motive for doing something is fear then it is wrong. Think again. What is the fear? Where is it coming from? What is the worst that can happen?

The opposite of fear is trust. Trust God. Trust the healing process. Trust your gut. Trust your heart, your true self lives here.

"TRAP"

WEEK 2

"A little sleuth work is in order to restore the persons we have abandoned – ourselves."

JULIA CAMERON

"But we return again and again to the still centre of our being, where the presence of God can be known."

Leaflet: 'YOUR FIRST QUAKER MEETING?'

"The still centre of our being." Where is that? We all have it. Therein lies the answers. Therein lies the presence of God within us. Therein lies our true selves. What stops us from reaching it? Distraction. We are distracted by ceaseless physical activity, by overloaded mental or intellectual activity, by strong emotions, by strong sensory input such as noise, bright lights, strong colours, physical discomfort.

How do we get there? By reducing the distractions, either in solitude or with a group. Groups who get together to pray, to meditate, to worship God, to break the hold of an addiction, all help. Strong emotions need to be expresses or released in a healthy way. Anger needs to be released, fear felt and grief poured out. Suppressed emotions block clarity of mind and feed into distractions.

"Rage, my love, against time's slow wire – old age strides us young. Resist, resist, them dark forces without."

CATHAL BROWNE

What are dark forces? They are forces of destruction, distraction, disease and disruption. These dark forces are without and within.

What is without? Without us is the air. In the air is oxygen which we need. There are also other substances which are not for our benefit; dust particles, pollutants from fossil fuels, emissions from factories and even some harmful rays from the sun.

There is also a great deal of information bouncing about from mobile phones, satellites, radio stations and TV from source to recipient.

There is also everything we take in through our mouths: food, drink and medicines. How much of that is destructive and contributes to disease?

There is everything we take in through our skin and all the rest of our senses. What do we look at that has a disruptive effect? What do we listen to that has a negative effect? Most important of all is what do we take into our minds, from whatever channel, that has a destructive effect?

"Resist, resist them dark forces without"!

"So with you, and I lay it on you as a command – no looking back. Give yourself, and all you ever met a fresh start from today."

TWO LISTENERS

If you feel guilty, look at it honestly. Did you do something wrong or not? If you have admit it to yourself, to another human being and make amends it possible. Now, once that is out of the way; no looking back, no holding on to shame or regret. Today is the first day of the rest of your life. Let go of all resentments, all hatred, all bad feeling, all self reproach, all doubt and all fear. Go forward fearlessly into the future.

Let go of all worry. Launch out into the deep. Trust. Trust. Trust. God is with you. God will support you in what ever you do that is right for you. You will be led, guided in the right direction. God does love you. You are very precious in His eyes. Every hair of your head is counted. Every moment of your life is cherished. Every aspect of your being is clearly understood. You are loved, so go forward unafraid.

"It is not circumstances that need altering first, but ourselves, and then the conditions will naturally alter."

TWO LISTENERS

Is this true? If it is, it is amazing. This means, if we are in difficulties or difficult circumstances we must first look to ourselves. What part am I playing in this situation? Am I reacting to other people's actions, threats or intimidations? Am I paralyzed into inaction or are other people pulling my chain? Am I full of ingratitude? Is there anything to be grateful for in my current circumstances? What are my strengths? What do I have power over? I have power over myself, that is my own actions and my reactions to others.

"Who will set a guard on my mouth, and an efficient seal on my lips, to keep me from falling, and my tongue from causing my ruin?"

ECCLESIASTICUS 22:27

There is a time to speak and a time to stay silent. Therein lies wisdom, knowing what to say and when to say it. Some people talk too much, constantly chattering but not really saying what needs to be said. Words are powerful. In the story of the *Emperor's New Clothes*, the child spoke up and stated the obvious. He spoke the truth that nobody wanted to hear.

Words can be used to distract from the truth or to pinpoint the truth. Words can be used to hurt or to heal, to cause trouble or to bring peace. Positive words can uplift, negative words bring us down.

Words are powerful, hand over your mouth to God, before you speak.

"Therefore all must be the better for coming in contact with both of you, because you are channels. See this, and you will think it natural to know they are being helped, not by you, but by My Spirit flowing through you as a channel."

TWO LISTENERS

"My Spirit", here is God's spirit. When you open yourselves to God's spirit, it flows through you like a river. You will be used to help others, even without knowing it. The light of life will shine through you. Those who want it will be attracted to you, those who do not want it, will be repelled by you and hate you. Hatred, malice and every evil spirit will come flying at you and your family. You will need protection. Pray for protection for yourself, your family, all who live with you, all in your complex, all in your neighbourhood and your country.

You can ask God to give you protection. You can ask all the members of your family tree, who are now with God to pray for you. You can ask Mary, the mother of Jesus to wrap her mantle of protection around you and those you are praying for. You can ask the archangel Michael, to stand guard over the people and places you are praying for.

You can ask for protection for all means of transportation you or those you care for use. That is every train, bus, plane, car or bicycle you or yours use. You can ask, your patron saint, your guardian angel and all the saints and angels in heaven to pray for you and with you.

"SHANDON"

WEEK 3

"A tittle-tattler lets secrets out, the trustworthy keeps things hidden."

PROVERBS 11:13

"If you learn to love yourself, and believe that you deserve the goodness life has to offer, then, you will attract loving people to you."

WAKTER RINDER

This is huge. "If you love yourself." How can you learn to love yourself if you have not been loved as a child? Is not life a search for love lost, love never given or love never received? Is not this the huge pain of life? Babies are born so close to perfection. They have an absolute expectation of perfect love. They cry and no one answers. They are hungry and no one feeds them. They long for human contact and they are left alone. They need order and they get chaos. They need to explore and they are restricted. They are put down and again and again.

Yet God is but a heartbeat away. Love is very close. Love conquers all, if you let it. So let love blossom. Let love blossom and love yourself. Let the small kernel of love within receive the nourishment from love without; from other people or directly from the Spirit of God, and let it blossom and grow.

Love yourself. Love yourself enough not to condemn yourself. Love yourself enough to take care or yourself, mind, body, and spirit. Love yourself enough to give yourself time off. Love yourself enough to have fun, to let off steam, to laugh and to enjoy what is beautiful.

"My love, which neither sea nor land, nor death itself, can extinguish or lessen towards you, most endearingly visits you with eternal embraces, and will abide with you for ever."

WILLIAM PENN

William Penn wrote this to his wife and children before embarking on a long and dangerous journey. These are beautiful words. Whom do I love like this? Is there anyone who loves me like this?

I believe that God loves me like this but it is hard to fully accept it. The Bible says that God loves me, that I am precious in his eyes and that every hair on my head is counted. Progressing from believing it to knowing it is a long slow process. To really know that I am loved is difficult. God does love me no matter what I do, however he can only work in my life if I surrender my life and my will to him. The more I surrender, the more God takes care of me. He seems to be always saying "Trust me, trust me, trust me."

"Happiness is when what you think, what you say, and what you do are in harmony."

MAHATMA GANDHI

This is difficult. It is easy to think abstractly about something and do nothing constructive about it. You may say what you think and do not follow it through. You may say one thing and do another.

Where does this unity of being come from? Does thinking come first? Some people just do the right thing in a situation apparently without thinking. It could be that they just think a little and then act. Obsessive thinking or over analyzing is a block to appropriate action. Too much analyzing after an event or action is a block to thinking and acting in the present.

Being alive in the present is what brings about harmony. Being where you are now. Feeling at ease with yourself, being alert to what is going on around you; these are the things that bring about harmony in mind and body.

To be at ease with yourself, you need to clear away all obsessive thinking and conflicting emotions. Conflicting emotions are often buried strong emotions, thoughts and images. How can you do all that? You can do it with God's help, working directly or through other people. Surrender your life and your will to God and all will work out for the best in time.

"He was suddenly surprised with an inward comfort, and as he thought an external glory in the room, which gave rise to religious emotions, during which he had the strongest convictions of the being of a God, and that the soul of man was capable of enjoying communion with Him."

WILLIAM PENN

William Penn founded Pennsylvania in the US and was one of the early prominent Quakers. He was 13 when he had this conversion experience. This was while listening to another man speak of his own experiences.

Everything that children are exposed to is so important. Children and young people have open minds. Somewhere in the Bible it says "Suffer little children to come unto me, for theirs is the kingdom of heaven." They need protection from lies, from deceit and falsehoods of every kind. They need exposure to all that is good, to truth, to honesty, to kindness and to love.

The care of children is a most important and rewarding task. Those who care for children, also need to be protected and cared for, in order to be free to do this most important of jobs.

"Do not abandon your heart to grief, drive it away, bear your own end in mind."

ECCLESIASTICUS 38:20

This I think means that, there is a time for grieving and a time to let go of grief. Grieving is necessary and good but there comes a time when it can become destructive. You can wallow in it, get stuck in it, not want to come out of it. You need to lift yourself out of it or allow others to help you out of it. "Drive it away", this takes energy and effort. "Bear your own end in mind". This means that you can die too. It is possible to die from grief. Some people give up after the death of a loved one or someone they have come to depend on for some essential element of life. They believe that they can not live without the other.

God gives us people to help us through life. Some people cross our paths to teach us lessons that only they can teach us. Others are sent to help us along the road of life. Still others are sent to give us pleasure and delight, to lighten the burden of life. Only a baby in his or her mother's womb is totally dependant on another for survival. For the rest of us absolute dependence on another human being, is not from God or of God.

"I am with you, much with you both, not only at these times, at all times. Feel conscious of My Presence. Earth hath no greater joy than that."

TWO LISTENERS

The Two Listeners believed that God spoke directly to them. This is God saying to them, "I am with you". Do you believe this? Do we really believe God is with us? Throughout the Bible, God says it over and over again, to the Chosen People, to the Israelites in the Old Testament and to his disciples in the New Testament.

It is hard to believe it until we see little signs. Once I was going on a journey. I had very little money. When I counted my money, I saw that I was 1 cent short. I looked down on the ground. There was a 1 cent piece. I picked it up and said "Thank you God." It was a little reminder. It gave me a boost. God provided for me. God was with me then. He is with us today and every day.

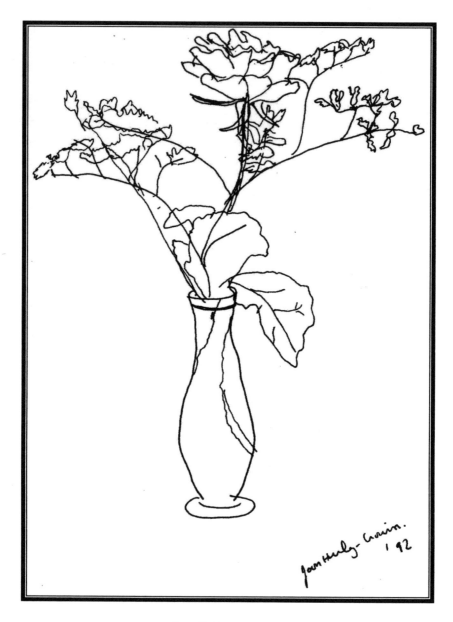

"LIFE"

WEEK 4

"In the things that really matter, life, love, reality, God, no one can teach you a thing."

ANTHONY DE MELLO

"I shall bring them down. Should they hide on the top of Carmel, I shall track them down and catch them."

AMOS 9:2-3

The "them" referred to here are those who believe in false gods. We can make a false god out of anything. Anything we believe we cannot live without. It could be that we believe we cannot live without sex: if we can have the best sex ever we will be extremely happy; that if we can have sex with him or her, life will be wonderful. Relationships can be another. If I can meet the perfect man / woman, life will be perfect. Money and possessions are another, the good income, perfect house, newest car and all will be well.

We are brought low by those and other false gods. Sex can be wonderful but then the feeling passes and you want more and more. The perfect relationship can turn into a nightmare or the mundane and ordinary. Possessions satisfy for a short time but then there is disenchantment and a search for more.

In the natural order of things you need to go down to come up. In the spiritual dimension you also need to reach a point of despair, of utter hopelessness, a sense of your own inability to cope before you surrender to God, before you reach out and ask him for help. Then the dawn breaks and help comes in the morning.

"Money is God in manifestation as freedom from want and limitation, but it must be always kept in circulation and put to right uses."

FLORENCE SCOVEL SHINN

Money is absolutely essential for life nowadays. Without our own money or someone else's we would die. Money is a supply. God is providing this supply. We are given money to use it and not hoard it. Money is also movement. Without money we cannot move about. Money flows. It flows in and out. It freezes. It evaporates. Hoarding is wrong and envying other people's possessions is wrong. We are given money for our own use, to supply our own needs and others. So use it. Spend as you go. Spend as you need. Give generously to others with discretion as they need it. Be a great giver. Let money flow out freely and more will flow in to replace it.

"Once more I say, tell them (his children)it is my counsel they should be tender and affectionate one to another."

WILLAM PENN

How can you be "tender and affectionate", if you are cross, irritable and tired? You cannot. If you are tired you need rest. If you are hungry you need to eat. If you are in physical pain you need medical help. If you are in emotional pain you need to release it. Before you can be "tender and affectionate" to others, you need to be "tender and affectionate" to yourself. Treat yourself well. Get yourself out of stressful situations. Give yourself the gift of time. Take time to have a bath, to do your hair, to go for a walk, to read the paper or tidy up your tool box. Take time to talk to God everyday.

Look after your health. Have a good food day. Go for a cycle or a boat ride. Go to the beach or up a mountain or down by the river. Be good to yourself and life will be good to you. Give out tenderness and affection and it will come back to you a thousandfold.

"Drive fear and depression and despair and a sense of failure out with Praise."

TWO LISTENERS

The "Praise" referred to here is praising God. If you do not believe or acknowledge God, look for all the good in your life, all the good things in the present. I am alive, I can walk, I can see and I can hear. Make a list. I can read and write. My children are alive and well. I have contact with them. Just for today I have a place to stay, clothes to wear and food to eat. Look at all the good and necessary things in your life. Look at all the people in your life that are good to you or good for you in any way. Look at all the good non-essential things, like recorded music, pictures and flowers. Have you smelt a rose lately? Look for all the beautiful priceless things like a sunset, a smile, the sight of a child asleep, the smell of roses or lilies, the flight of birds, the flow of a river and the drift of clouds.

"Be strong and show yourself a man. Observe the injunction of Yahweh your God, following his ways and keeping his laws…, so that you may be successful in everything you do and undertake."

KINGS 2:2 – 3

"Be strong and show yourself a man." Who nowadays asks us to "be strong"? It seems to me that we are asked to be clever, be cunning, be selfish, be fashionable, be cool, be slick, be modern, be with it or be hip. But to "be strong" is to stand out, to stand up for something. It means to say no to wrong doing, to corruption, to deceit and to lies. It means to stand for the truth and not to compromise with evil.

When you are standing up for the truth and not compromising with evil then you are automatically "following his (God's) ways". God is our creator. He made us to follow his ways. We all know deep down when we have done something wrong, something which is against our very nature. There is a voice in us that cries out "no! no!". We have a conscience. Use it. Be your true self. "Be strong and show yourself a man".

"Regret nothing not even the sins and failures."
TWO LISTENERS

Everything that happens in life has a purpose. Good can come from all situations. You can learn from everything. You can grow from all situations. The thing is to learn your lesson quickly and move on. If you do not learn your lesson, it will be repeated over and over again, in different situations.

Good can come from all situations, if you surrender that situation to God. Ask God to enter it and to enter you. It is very difficult to see, while you are in a challenging place, what good will come of it. It is during these times that you need to trust and pray and ask others to pray for you. That is why it is good to pray in a group. Groups can pray for you and with you, for each other and with each other. Others can pray for you even when you cannot pray for yourself.

Trust that all will be well. Say it over and over again: "All is well". "If God is with me, who can be against me? No one!"

"KATE"

WEEK 5

"When fear is in control, fight or flight are our only options. More often than not, we choose flight and scurry off to one of our numerous hiding places."

EARNIE LARDEN & CAROL LARSEN HEGARTY

33

"When life seems hard, and troubles crowd, then very definitely look for causes for thankfulness."

TWO LISTENERS

At times like this you need to start making a list either verbally to someone else or in writing. Write down everything you are grateful for. Like being alive, your loved ones being alive; all your abilities; your ability to walk, to talk, to see, for all the people that are good and supportive to you, for the weather, for protection from disasters and disease; for living to this moment; for protection from all the things that could be worse.

When you focus on the positive the negative shrinks back to a manageable size. Just for today you need to accept things as they are. Change can come tomorrow.

"Do not be too ready to do, just be. I said, 'be ye therefore perfect,' not 'do' perfect things."

TWO LISTENERS

Being is more important than doing. Be in the present, be alive, and be alert. Bring yourself into the present. Stop, listen, what can you hear? Traffic, birds singing, people talking, doors slamming. Look around you. What do you see? A room, a picture, people on the bus? How does your body feel? Do you have any aches, any pains anywhere? Do you feel the pressure of the ground on your feet? Do you feel the pressure of the chair against you back? How is your breathing? Are you holding unto your breath? Do you need to take a few deep breaths? If so breathe out all your negativity, let it all go out. Now breathe in slowly all the good things of life. How does your mouth feel? How do you feel emotionally now? Tension, fear, panic, hysteria, guilt, peace, love, anger, sorrow or joy? Allow yourself to feel your feeling. What is your feeling connected to? You have a lifelong journey to know yourself; start now.

"If we are facing in the right direction, all we have to do is to keep on walking."

BUDDIST SAYING

"If you are facing the right direction," well that is the problem. How do we know that we are facing in the right direction? You may pray for guidance but sometimes it is not clear. Sometimes you just have to try things out for yourself and see what happens. If things are not going well, if everything seems to be difficult, it could be an indication that you are on the wrong path. If you are on the right path things usually work out, the money comes in, the help comes in, and the direction becomes clear. If the road you are on is of great spiritual value to yourself or others, then initially there is a lot of opposition, but something will let you know that you are on the right path. Sometimes a moment of vision, of clarity, comes when you see clearly the direction you must go in. Hold the vision. Write it down. Keep on going in that direction. Keep the focus on what you are doing and you will get there eventually.

"Kind words can be short and easy to speak, but their echoes are endless."

MOTHER THERESA OF CALCUTTA

Yes, kindness is the mightiest force. Kindness is never forgotten. True kindness is unselfish and seeks only to love and heal, never looks for its own reward. When all the dust settles, it's the kind deeds that stand out in the landscape of life. I once was very short of money and went to sell some important jewelry. By the time I got to the tenth jeweller I got a sale and was crying uncontrollably. The lady slipped an extra $50 from her own purse into a paper hanky and gave it to me with the sale price. This act of kindness I will always remember along with many other acts of kindnesses I have received along the way of life.

"Dwell in my Love. Laugh and trust. Laughter is a child's faith in God and good."

TWO LISTENERS

Laughter is good. Laughter is healing. Laughter releases tension in your body. You can only laugh when you feel safe. In a cinema chair or a home sofa, you can watch someone make a complete fool of themselves and laugh because you are completely safe. It does not involve you personally in any way. When you laugh until you cry there is a great release and healing takes place. Laughter brings you into the present, it releases tension and it lets go of inhibitions. Children, who are well cared for and feel safe in their homes with their families, can laugh easily.

God cares about you, today, now. You are safe. God is with you. Trust God. Trust goodness. Trust nature. Let God's protective arm surround you.

"When the upright are on the increase, the people rejoice; when the wicked are in power, the people groan."

PROVERBS 29:2

This is so true. Every decision made by the people in power affects us all. There are people in every country and the world as a whole, who between them have the political, legal and economic power. Their decisions affect us all whether we know of them or not. When decisions are made for the common good, the whole community can relax and prosper. The wicked make decisions for their own benefit solely. This helps a tiny minority to prosper at the expense of the majority. Then the people groan, maybe not immediately but eventually when the changes start to affect them. They may not even be aware of what is affecting them, just that what used to be simple is now complicated, what used to be comfortable is now stressful. What used to be possible is now extremely difficult or totally impossible. We need to pray for the people in power, the people with the real earthly power (not just those who seem to have it) all the time.

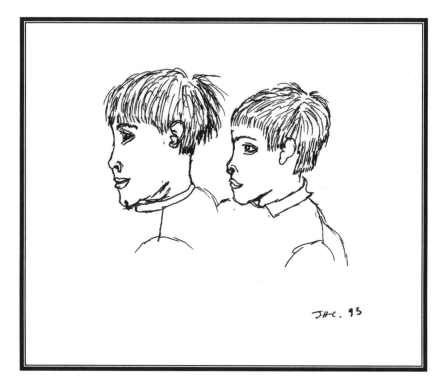

"JAMES AND TOMAS"

WEEK 6

"Proper punctuation is both the sign and the cause of clear thinking."

LYNNE TRUSS

"Over and over again man is told to 'stand still'."
FLORENCE SCOVEL SHINN

Standing still is letting go and not trying to force solutions. You do what you can and let God do the rest. You surrender the situation into God's care and await instructions, acting only when you are prompted. This is very difficult. Fear, anxiety and guilt get in the way. "I should be doing this or that or the other". Let go, let go, let go, trust God. The right answer is there but you will not hear it until you are calm. Put yourself back into God's care. Take a bath, go for a walk or a run, a cycle or a climb. When you are calm and still the answer will come. Sometimes the answer is do nothing. So do nothing for now.

"God's will be done, not man's, God's pattern, not man's pattern, is the command we find running through all the scriptures."

FLORENCE SCOVEL SHINN

It is God's will for us and God's pattern in our own lives we need to seek. But first we need to surrender our lives and our will to God as a lifelong commitment. Then continue this as a daily practice. When we are in his care, ask for the 'divine design' of our lives to manifest. That is, what is right for you to do, just you. Everybody has special talents, things that are really easy for them to do; things that feel more like play than work. This is where you should be. Go where your talent leads you. It is where you are meant to be. If you get a glimpse of a life that seems to be too good to be true, go for it. It is for you. It is where you are meant to be. Take the opportunity when it comes. Walk through the door when it opens. Fear not. God is with you. All is well.

"In fact, active faith is the bridge, over which man passes to his Promised Land."

FLORENCE SCOVEL SHINN

Believe and trust. Believe that God is with you. Trust him to be there for you. Act as if all is well and it will be. The supply will be met. What you need will be supplied. Do not act poor. Act rich. God is rich. He loves to give. He loves you and he will supply all your needs. Ask for what you need and would like and act as if you have it already. Do not hold unto money. Keep a prudent reserve, pay your bills when due, then spend freely. Be generous, believing that God will always supply your needs. Do not hold back. Bravely face the future, all you need is there already. Believe and trust.

"As water reflects face back to face, so one human heart reflects another."

PROVERBS 27:19

We attract the people and situations into our lives that we need. That is, the people we need to learn from. If we are reacting strongly to some person or situation, we need to stand back and ask what is going on here for me? What is it about this person or situation that I am reacting to? The other person could be showing you an aspect of yourself, you do not like. Change can only come from within, within yourself. You are the one in your life that can change. You will be given this power if you ask for it. If you change how you react to a situation, the situation itself will change.

"Never turn your face from the poor and God will never turn his from you."

TOBIT 4:7

Who are the "poor"? All who do not have what they currently need. Those who do not have sufficient or adequate accommodation, food, medical care, protection, fresh air, exercise, leisure, love, guidance or respect, are the poor; all who are lacking in any way; lacking judgment, knowledge, clarity or insight. Those who lack the basic practical necessities of life or the basic spiritual ones are the poor.

What does it mean to "turn your face away"? It means to ignore, to harden your heart, to look the other way, to disregard.

The thing to ask is: what is the real need in the situation? What is really needed here? Children may ask for material goods but need a hug or boundaries set or discipline. An adult may be looking for sex but need reassurance, to be told no, not now, not appropriate or not with me. Some needs are simple. If a person is homeless they need accommodation. If they are hungry they need food. Some are not so easy to discern. Pray for guidance.

"I waited all day for you. I waited longer. The sun had gone down on our love. I waited on."

CATHAL BROWNE

Waiting. Waiting can be so difficult. Will it happen or won't it? Will she come or won't she come? Will I be all right or won't I be all right? Is all well or is it not? Doubt and fear, they are the two enemies of peace, of love, true love, real love. The only answer to doubt and fear is belief and trust. Trust God. Trust the process. Trust your gut feeling. Believe that God is with you. Believe that you are protected. Believe that you are precious in God's eyes. Believe you are in God's care. Believe that you will be taken care of. All is well. Say "All is well", all is well, all is well".

"WATERFALL"

WEEK 7

"We enjoy the freedom of adulthood and the pleasures of childhood if we remain young at heart."

LYNDA FIELD

"Finally, stick to the advice your heart gives you, no one can be truer to you than that."

ECCLESIASTICUS 37:13

Deep in your own heart are all your answers. God dwells within. God lives there. Some people call it their gut. A good question to ask is "what does my gut say?"

How can you get deep into your own heart? First you must still the Chatterbox. The Chatterbox is the record or records that keep going around in your head. You can do this by prayer, by meditation, by bringing yourself into the present, by being still. Then ask your heart what is right for you, in the situation. Your answer will come, in time.

"As for me, if I lie down and sleep,
I shall awake, for Yahweh sustains me.
I have no fear of people in their thousands upon thousands,
who range themselves against me wherever I turn."

PSALMS 3:5 – 6

This may seem paranoid but it was a reality for King David at that time. Today there is a great deal of malice, hatred, ill will, suspicion, prying, spying and a huge lack of personal privacy. "I have no fear of people," David said. David turned to God, to protect him and help him. In David's time, the Israelites called God the Creator of heaven and earth Yahweh. Today we need protection every bit as much as David did. We need protection for our families and our country, from evil, ill will, disease and disaster. We can put ourselves, our families and our country into the hands of God daily and we will be protected daily. Whenever fear comes upon you ask God for protection and you will get it, for yourselves, or for others.

"Man receives only that which he gives. The Game of life is a game of boomerangs."

FLORENCE SCOVEL SHINN

This is true. What you give out you get back but not always from the same person or source. You give out love to one person but it can come back through another person.

Negative boomerangs can also reverberate down through the generations. Ill will, hatred, malice, murder and curses going out from one of your ancestors can come back to affect you. You can be affected by the behaviour and spirit of an ancestor back seven generations. That is why you or somebody else on your behalf, needs to pray for all members of your family tree on both sides – the natural mother's and father's – back seven generations and down to the present day.

Prayer is needed to neutralize the effects of all curses made by your ancestors and on your ancestors. Prayer is also needed to neutralize and dissipate all the effects of major sins by and upon all members of your family tree. Murder, sexual assault, Satanic worship and occult practices are all major sins because they always have a negative, destructive effect. Prayer is also needed for all the physical remains of your ancestors and all the grounds they have ever rested in.

"Love is a great thing, a good above all others, which alone maketh every burden light."

THOMAS Á KEMPIS

Unless you have known and experienced love it means nothing. Where does love come from? It comes from God, directly or through other people. Can it come through nature?

I believe it can. God's spirit is in nature, the spirit of love, of power and of truth. The further we get from nature, the further we get from God. Nature works in harmony and balance. Abundance is the natural way. Left to its own devices nature will provide abundance, variety and interest in all of its expressions: in animals, plants, pure water, clean air, beautiful scenery on land, sea and air. Nature also keeps its jewels, its secrets and its treasures hidden deep; deep within the earth, deep within ourselves, deep within the soil, or deep within each individual cell.

Allow love to surround you like the waters of a warm lake. It is there for us. Ask for it. Go out into the air and sunshine and know that God is with you. God is in the air that caresses your skin. God is in the sun that warms your body. God is in the leaf that gives out pure air. God is in the face of a flower that enchants you. God is in the birds as they sing for you, talking to you telling you "I am here, I am here, life is good, look up to the sky."

"He who sheds the blood of man, by man shall his blood be shed, for in the image of God was man created."

GENESIS 9:6

Killing is always wrong. Killing another human being has far reaching consequences, for both the killer and the victim. The victim's life has been taken and all their future children and their descendants are wiped out. It causes spiritual death to the killer. Without healing and forgiveness, it can affect the next seven generations of the killer's family tree. We need to pray for all members of our family tree who have committed murder either deliberately or unintentionally. We also need to pray for their victim's family tree.

"To love at all is to be vulnerable."

C S LEWIS

To love is to open your heart. When your heart is open a knife can be stuck in it. But when your heart is open you can not be deliberately cruel , cold or indifferent. An open heart sees others clearly, feels pain, compassion and great joy. A baby's heart is open. Pain can close it down. Our wounded hearts can open again when we are in the presence of love. For some this comes from a lover, or a group of people, or directly from God. For some people the first time, as an adult, their heart opens is when they hold and accept their child for the first time, whether it is their natural child or one that has come to them as a gift. That is why, I believe, the forces of darkness hate children and constantly work to stop us having natural children or accepting other children into our lives fully.

"WILTING"

WEEK 8

"Few of us really know about love or friendship
but Bonding is what we do in spite of ourselves."

JAMES KELLY

"When we forgive someone, the knots are untied and the past is released."

RESHAD FIELD

This is true. Forgiveness is a process of letting go, letting go of the past, letting go of injuries, letting go of resentment, letting go and releasing anger. Forgiveness is not an act of will, but a process, a healing process. For this you need grace or spiritual power, the power of God working for you, in you. Grace is a free gift form God, unmerited. All you have to do is ask for it, or someone else can ask for you. You can also ask for grace for someone else. All healing takes place through grace, sometimes slowly sometimes quickly. When two or more people get together and pray for someone or some situation, the grace increase is manifold. Small group prayer is very powerful especially if they concentrate on praying for specific people or situations.

"That it will never come again is what makes life so sweet."
                                        EMILY DICKINSON

      Yes and painful and difficult and challenging. We do not know if life will come again. Some believe it will. But we do not know it. We know we are alive now. We know this is our own life until our own death. Now is the moment. Now is the reality. This is it. This is life. Maybe it is as good as it gets. Live in the moment. Look around you. Are there signs of life, of love, of happiness, of humour anywhere? Focus your attention on all the good there is to see, to feel, to smell, to touch and to hear. Be here now. Don't anticipate, just be today.

DAY 3   WEEK 8   FEBRUARY 21

"Fret not your soul with puzzles that you cannot solve."
                                    TWO LISTENERS

There are some questions that have no answers. There are some questions that we are not ready or able to understand the answers to. There are some questions that are not right for us to know the answers too. There are many questions that are the wrong ones for us to ask. It is not our business to know why so and so did such and such to us. The question is why did I react in such a way to this? Why am I reacting so strongly to this? What in me is being triggered by this? We will find the answer to the puzzle of ourselves. Focusing on others is a distraction.

"He who smiles rather than rages is always stronger."

JAPANESE PROVERB

There is a place for rage but not against the innocent. Our tendency is to dump rage on our nearest and dearest, our children, our life or our employees. Anyone who is close to us and who will not answer back on the spot. This is not right. They do not deserve it. The outward reason for the rage is often an excuse, not the true reason. Any one who rages can ask what really triggered that? Why did I lose it? What was it about, that situation that triggered the rage? There is something in the past, some deep hurt or injury, triggering the current situation. Track the rage to its source. Release it in a healthy way. If you can not do this on your own, ask God to help you. The help will come either from God directly or from people. Once you track it to its source, you will be able to release it in a healthy way. Very often it will dissolve in tears.

"There is a place he is to fill and no one else can fill, something he is to do, which no one else can do."
FLORENCE SCOVEL SHINN

This is great. This means that everyone is special. Everyone has something unique to give to the world, the world they find themselves in. This in turn affects the whole world. Everything we do is important. Everything we say or think has an effect. The effect is either positive or negative. One kind word, one kind gesture can have a knock-on effect like a stone thrown into a lake, the ripples extend far and wide. A smile, a small gift, a curtsy, a helping hand, everything matters. Everything matters and everybody is special, unique, important.

"Yahweh gave Solomon wisdom as he had promised him; good relations persisted between Solomon and Hiram, and the two of them concluded a treaty."

1 KINGS 5:26

Wisdom is needed to have good relations. Where does wisdom come from? It comes from God. True wisdom is clarity of mind and heart. It is being able to see into the heart of the matter. So often fear controls people and situations. Good agreements satisfy all parties to the agreement, fears are relieved and justice is done. Wisdom allows you to see through a situation to what is really going on, to perceive the true agendas of all parties concerned. A balance of power is needed for the common good. A good agreement leaves both parties feeling that they have and actually are, doing well out of the agreement.

Surrender all disagreements to God. Pray for clarity and wisdom to guide your own behavior through this matter. Sometimes agreements can not be reached and wisdom will guide you to withdraw from the conflict.

"THE ABBOT"

WEEK 9

"For o'er and o'er again this evening's dancing
I'll dance with you in memory's hall,
And feel your whispers on my cheek
And the rebel curls that fall."

MAX EHRMANN

"No man is your enemy, no man is your friend, every man is your teacher."

AUTHOR UNKNOWN

This is so true. Everybody you met or have contact with is there for a reason. Especially those that aggravate, annoy, frighten or even terrify us. People are put in our paths for a reason. They are there, to provide an opportunity for our growth. We may not take this opportunity but it is there for us.

The real question is not, why is this happening to me, or why are they doing this to me, but what can I learn from this person or situation? What are they triggering in me that makes me react in this way? Is this a warning to me saying do not do this or do not go there? Does this person need to be prayed for?

Bless everybody you meet or have contact with. Baptize everything that happens to you a success. Therein lies true freedom.

"Wait to hear My Will and then obey. At all costs obey."
TWO LISTENERS

This is really difficult. How do you know what is God's will and what is man's? First things first. Are you willing to do God's will in all things or in just some things or in nothing at all? If you are willing even a little bit, then you need to hand over your life and your will to the care of God. This you need to do now, and every day from now on, and every time doubt or fear assails you.

Back to the question, what is God's will for us? It is sometimes very difficult to know except that, when you are on the right track then peace comes. There are also moments of absolute clarity. This is the time to write it down, so that you can look back on it in moments of doubt. When you are in doubt ask God to show you the way and to let you know you are on the right path. Peace will come. Things will work out in a marvellous way, miracles do happen, the sun shines after the rain and calm comes after the storm.

Go forward bravely into the night and all will be revealed, step by step, action by action, a little at a time, one day at a time.

"There is no path greater than love.
There is no law higher than love.
And there is no beyond love.
God and love are identical."

MEHER BABA

To love is to open your heart. Once your heart is open, you can be hurt. Love expands and fear contracts. Love brings you out of yourself and beyond. It opens your mind and your heart. It clears your senses. You can see, hear, smell and touch more clearly and distinctly. This can be very painful. It can leave you open to deep hurt.

Babies come into the world with an open mind and heart. They take everything in. They respond naturally. There are no barriers to their complete feelings. They trust completely. When their trust is betrayed, their heart is wounded. They start to shut down their hearts, their minds and their senses.

Healing is needed. Protection is needed. Healing comes with an opening up, an opening up to sorrow and pain, to anger and loss. These are the poisons that need to be relieved. Fear is the enemy of love. Fear and love can not exist together. Fear keeps the poison in place. Fear contracts, love expands. Pray for love. Pray much for love to enter your being.

"Do not gaze at wine-----
In the end its bite is like a serpent's,
its sting as sharp as an adder's."

PROVERBS 23:31 – 32

Alcoholism is a very destructive disease. A disease is something which causes disease, ill ease, something that is not working right. Alcoholism destroys the individual and all the people surrounding the alcoholic, all who are intimately connected with him or her. Alcoholism can only be maintained by constant lies and distortions of the truth. It is a vortex of lies, distortions, deceits, blame and counter blame. The truth is the addiction has taken hold of the individual alcoholic and that is what must be dealt with. The alcoholic blames those, closest to him or her, for his or her state; they in turn blame others, or, take the blame on board themselves as shame. Within the morass of lies and deceit is fear, fear of exposure, fear of the truth or fear of the consequences of exposure. The spiritual answer is the only effective one.

"Without stirring abroad one can know the whole world.
Without looking out the window one can see the way to heaven.
The further one goes the less one knows."

LAO TZU

What does this mean? "Without stirring abroad one can know the world"! The whole world is within. God is within and through God we are connected to the whole world. All we need to do is make contact with the God within.

How do you do that? This is a difficult one. First, you need to eliminate anything that truly distracts your attention. You know yourself what that is for you. It could be your phone, your computer, the television, the radio or your children. Second you need to calm your body. It is a question of what works for you. For some people it is perhaps, sitting still with your back straight and your feet planted firmly on the ground. For others it is lying down or kneeling down or being immersed in water. For others it could be a rhythmical activity, like walking, cycling, running, swimming or drumming, that calms the body and frees the mind. Thirdly, we all have the Chatterbox going on in our head. This needs to be stilled. Some people repeat a prayer, a mantra or an affirmation. This helps stop the chatterbox and calms the mind. Some people find deep regular breathing calming for both mind and body. What ever works, do it.

When your body and mind is calm then you can listen to the still calm voice within. Ask for what ever you need or would like. If you would like, clarity or guidance or supply of any kind ask for it. Ask and you will receive.

"Expect a miracle for a week. Wholeheartedly believe that one will happen and keep trusting. The miracle might not be the one you are expecting but I can assure you something amazing will happen."

LYNDA FIELD

Belief is the most powerful medicine of all. Believe that you can be healed and will be healed and you will be. Believe that you deserve the best that life has to offer and you will get it. Believe that God is there for you and you will know it. God is always with us, but for us to know it, to feel it we need to believe.

Believe that you are a good and talented person and you will be. Believe that all that has happened to you in your life to date has a purpose and that good will come of it and it will. Believe that you will get the best accommodation, the best work, the best relationships and the best health and it will happen. It will all come about in time and in a perfect way.

Doubt and fear are the enemy. Attack them virulently. They are your greatest enemy. Get support from other like-minded people and keep the flag flying. The flag of hope, trust and love.

"MAN SMOKING"

WEEK 10

"You got used to it. In fact, it wasn't too bad. You just had to fill in your day, and that wasn't all that hard really."

RODDY DOYLE

"Paddy would, of course, be buried near his parents in his native townland, but his relatives had decided that since he lived here so long the funeral Mass should be held here."

CATHAL BROWNE

He "would, of course, be buried near his parents." How wonderful to have a place to be buried in, waiting for you when you need it and to be absolutely assured of it. This privilege is not available to everyone nowadays.

Respect for the dead, their remains and where their remains are to be laid to rest is very important. Different cultures and religion traditions have different rituals and ways of dealing with the dead and their remains. Whatever tradition is followed there is one thing in common, that is the belief that, if the dead and their remains are not treated with respect then there are huge spiritual consequences to the dead and their living relatives. Some North American Indian tribes scalped the dead in the belief that it allowed their spirit to be released from their body, freeing them to enter the spirit world.

Cannibalism was a deliberate attempt to desecrate the dead of their enemies. The cannibals believed that if some of their enemies' flesh were eaten, then the dead could not enter the spirit world as their spirit would be absorbed into them and that the body and the spirit of their enemy would then be completely destroyed.

"Let's face the music and dance."

IRVING BERLIN

This is lovely. To face the music is to face your fears and to deal with difficult situations head on. Fear is the enemy. Fear must be faced and dealt with every time it comes up. Fear is not from God. Fear contracts and love expands. Face the fear. What are you afraid of? Is the fear stopping you from doing something? How important is it? Do you need to do it? If so, feel the fear and just do it.

Dance. How wonderful it is. Light, harmonious, fun, joy, all rolled into one. Live in the moment. Enjoy everything. Take all the good things that are there to enjoy and enjoy them. Do a summersault. Be yourself. Leave all fear and doubt behind you. Bounce and play. Laugh, sing and dance. Joy. Joy. Joy.

"There is a place that you are to fill and no one else can fill, something you are to do, which no one else can do. There is a perfect picture of this in the super - conscious mind. It usually flashes across the conscious as an unattainable ideal – something too good to be true."

FLORENCE SCOVEL SHINN

Right so, if you have had any flash of anything that is "too good too be true", then that is for you. That is your perfect self expression.

God wants only perfection for us, perfect love, perfect health, perfect prosperity or supply of all our needs and perfect self expression. But in order to gain these things we need to ask God for them and believe that we deserve them, that we can get them and we will get them, that we deserve the absolute best that life has to offer and that everybody else does too.

Life is full of abundance. The abundance is there. Abundance is the rule of nature. Nature left to its own devices always produces things in great abundance. It is man that has interrupted the supply. Nature is God's own creation. In nature we see the mind of God reflected.

All that we wish for, all that we would like will come to us at the perfect time and in a perfect way, if we ask for it and believe that we will get it.

"When that day comes, a fountain will be opened for the House of David and the inhabitants of Jerusalem, to wash sin and impurity away."

ZECHARIAH 13:1

A fountain "to wash sin and impurity away"! What is sin and impurity? Impurity is usually referring to sins of a sexual nature, to the abuse of your own or other people's sexuality. So what is sin? Sin is any destructive, behaviour, thought or action. Some destructive behaviours are obvious – killing people, damaging property or telling lies. Others are not so obvious – verbal abuse, subtle undermining of a person's confidence or self esteem, subtle menacing or threatening behaviours.

Certain thoughts can be destructive – thoughts of resentment, hatred, ill will, criticisms, condemnations and negative imaging. Negative imaging is using your imagination to imagine the worst – disease, disaster, bad luck or failure of any kind. The imaging facility can bring about the reality. Guard your mind. Do not let it dwell on thoughts of failure or disaster.

Some feelings can be destructive. Fear is destructive. There is only one fear which is positive, that is a short sharp fear which acts as a warning. It tells us to run, get out quick or don't go there. Otherwise fight fear. It is not from God. It wreaks havoc and destruction all round. All other feelings need to be experienced and expressed in a healthy way, otherwise they cause sickness in the body or the mind.

"He has no equal on earth, being created without fear.
He looks the haughtiest in the eye;
of all the lordly beasts he is king."

JOB 41:25 – 26

Fearlessness is a great quality. It is to be magnificent, courageous, and oh so audacious. To do what is right, without fear of the consequences. Fearlessness can only come with absolute trust and certainty, trust that you will be taken care of, certainty that what you are doing is right and that all will be well. "There is nothing to fear but fear itself." Whoever said that was speaking the truth.

"Fear not for I am with you," says the Bible. God is with us. God will take you by the hand and lead you through the days, the weeks and the months ahead. God is with you and will carry you over all the troubled waters of life, through all the storms and land you in a safe harbour.

If God is with us so who can prevail against us? No one.

"It was a truly dreadful retribution that visited Israel."

1 MACCABEES 1:64

Retribution is to get back whatever you deserve. We get back what we give out when we are not living under grace. Retribution really means punishment, just punishment. The Old Testament is the story of the relationship between God and his Chosen People. Over and over again in this story, if the Chosen People disobeyed God's commands, they were punished.

How does this relate to us today? How do we disobey God today? By turning away from him or more specially by not turning towards him. If we are not in the care of God, we are in a void, no love, no clarity, no care and no direction.

Outside God's care is confusion, darkness, malevolence, hatred, fear and cruelty. God has given us free will. We can freely choose to align our wills to his or not. Today you can allow God into your life or not. The choice is yours. Choose God.

"PREHISTORIC"

WEEK 11

"However peace is not simply the absence of war; it is a vision of human wholeness."

HARVEY GILLMAN

"I am asked, so often by my students, 'How can I get rid of fear?' I reply, 'By walking up to the thing you are afraid of.'"

FLORENCE SCOVEL SHINN

If you know what you are afraid of, good. Face that fear, go straight up to that thing you are afraid of, praying all the time.

Some times it is difficult to know, what you are afraid of. If you have a nameless dread or fear, what is first things first? Examine it. If it is a negative image or thought then you need to banish it from your consciousness immediately. Do not entertain it for one second more. These images of disease, failure or destruction, are not from God. They need to be stopped straight away. A nameless dread in the pit of your stomach needs to be looked at in greater depth. Is it a person you are afraid of? If so walk right up to that person, do not avoid them.

Is it poverty or lack you are afraid of? If so spend fearlessly, with wisdom. Do not hold back. Be generous with what you have got. Give, give, give. It will all come back to you a thousand fold.

"'Do not be afraid,' he said, 'You are a man specially chosen; peace be with you, play the man, be strong.'"

DANIEL 10:19

"Do not be afraid." Over and over again in the Bible, God says this. In this case, it was an angel speaking to Daniel. "Do not be afraid", fear is not from God. There is some mention of the fear of God in the Bible, but that is reverence, respect, awareness of God's power. It is also being under the law not grace. When you are under the law you suffer the consequences of all of your actions. Everything you give out comes back to you. Under grace all is forgiven. All the effects of past sins are dissolved and dissipated. Grace being a free gift you must ask for it. Freedom from fear is a grace. Ask God to remove fear and replace it with courage. Courage to face the day, courage to live; to face each situation life brings to us, to deal with it; courage to speak up, courage to stay quiet, courage to leave, courage to stay, courage to stand and fight, courage to stand and stay quiet, courage to enjoy what is beautiful and courage to be in the moment.

"You are a man specially chosen." We are all specially chosen, every man, woman and child of us. We have been chosen to live. We all have a reason, to be here and a purpose. Everyone has special talents given to them, which can be used for their own good and the good of the whole community of mankind. "peace be with you, - - -, be strong."

"Play the man." It is important for men to be men. When men are being men, women can be women and children can be children.

83

"As one door closes another opens. Look for the newly opening door, look for the silver lining."

LYNDA FIELD

No matter how bad a situation is, there is always some good in it. But you have to look for it. Make a list of all the things you are grateful for today. You are alive. That is something to be grateful for. Life is a gift, a gift from God. We cannot create life. The breath of life comes from God. As parents we act as channels for new life to enter into the world. We can block that channel or let it flow but we cannot create life. We can destroy life. We can work against it or with it. Every moment of every day we can either be creative or destructive. Everything starts in our minds and hearts and works outwards, in thoughts, in actions. Negative thoughts have a destructive effect. Positive thoughts have a creative effect.

Look into your heart. Guard your mind and your tongue.

"'Here comes another man running alone,' David said. 'He too is a bearer of good news.'"

2 SAMUEL 18:26

Good news! We all need good news, to know that all is well, that no matter what happens we will be all right; that after every dark night there will be a dawn of a new day. The 'good news' is that God is with us, that God loves us; that no matter how things may appear, God is working in it and good will come out of it, provided that you hand the matter over to God to take care of in the first place.

The good news is that: if we surrender our lives and our wills to God, then God will take care of us and that every aspect of our lives will improve, in time. This surrender to God or allowing God to work in our lives, is needed on a daily, hourly, moment by moment basis. Then, when all of the moments of your life are over, the final surrender of death will be into his arms, forever.

"Learn to make the very best use of your time; it is your most valuable resource."

LYNDA FIELD

Time is precious. Some of us are rich in time but poor in money or material passions. Who is the richer, the man with lots of money to spend but little or no time to spend it as he wishes or the man with lots of time but very little money to spend? I think the man with lots of time. What is the point in working hard all your life and leaving a rich widow behind? Or worse still, having all you worked for wiped out in some economic downturn or swindle?

The gift of time is precious however it comes. It may come as a result of illness, unemployment, bankruptcy, a windfall of money, retirement or pregnancy. However it comes it is good.

You have time to get to know yourself; time to be with your children, partner or parents; time to be good to yourself; time to indulge in creative activities; time to learn new skills; time to meet new and different people; time to get fresh air and exercise; time to paint the house, do the garden, clear out the garden shed or attic; time to rediscover the lost art of letter writing; time to listen to and talk to God.

"They shall dance in praise of his name,
Play to him on tambourines and harp."

PSALMS 149:3

Over and over again in the Psalms, God is praised. All over the Bible, we are asked to and encouraged to praise God. Praise God first. Praise God at all times and in every circumstance. Praise God and thank God in every circumstance. Thanking God is also encouraged. Thanking is expressing gratitude. To be grateful for something is to be aware that it is a gift; that it is good and freely given.

To praise is, to be aware of the wonder of something. How wonderful, how good, how marvellous this is. To praise is to see the good in something and to approve of it. God wants our thanks and our praise. He has asked for it. He likes it and sends it back to us. It has a most marvellous effect in a situation. Once you start thanking and praising God, you start to see all the good in the situation. Courage and strength enter in, resentment, fear and negative thinking all flee. Misplaced anger evaporates and true outrage returns. Freedom and joy enters in and finally peace prevails.

"JAZZ 11"

WEEK 12

"God showed that we suffer from two kinds of sickness: one of them is impatience or sloth, because we find our trouble and suffering a heavy burden to bear, and the other is despair, or doubtful fear."

JULIAN OF NORWICH

"Go forward. You are only beginning the new life together. Joy, joy, joy."

TWO LISTENERS

Moving forward is painful. Growth is always painful. We like to stand still, stay in a rut, keep to our comfort zone or wallow in our misery. Going forward is moving out of our comfort zone. Sometimes circumstances force us out; loss of a job, a drop in our income, the death of someone close or an ending to a sexual relationship. These are opportunities for growth. They may lead us to move to a new area, a new county, a new job or a new career or just a new way of living.

Sometimes restlessness or a desire to experience new things moves us forward. Sometimes our present circumstances are very bad for us. We may be living with extreme stress or lack or both, and something has to give. It could be your mind, your body or your emotions. You could have a breakdown. If you do, rejoice; it could be a breakthrough. Surrender your breakdown to God; surrender all your life and all your present circumstances. The way forward will appear. Take your courage into your hands and go forward bravely into the future. God will be with you all the way. Launch out into the deep and the safety net will appear.

"Do not let lechery and lust grip me,
do not leave me a prey to shameless desire."
ECCLESIASTICUS 23:6

We were given sexual desire mainly in order that we can come together to make babies. There are also other bonuses. There is the bonus of physical comfort. This can give reassurance and a sense of belonging. It can help establish and maintain an emotional bonding between the two people engaging in sexual contact. The final bonus is, of course, sensual pleasure leading to an intense climactic sensation, a peak sensual experience.

Lust, or lechery, enters in when we seek only the sexual climax. The more and more you indulge in it for its own sake, the harder it is to achieve and the less you are able to postpone gratification. Experimentation enters in and the object of desire can change: to other people's partners, to partners of the same sex, to children, to the use of objects, to animals or to achieving pain. These are the shameless desires.

"Having marched form Gilgal throughout the night, Joshua caught them unawares."
JOSHUA 10:9

God is with us in all our endeavours. We may not see it but he is working all the time for our benefit. In the dead of night the forces of good are working for us. They are working to destroy our enemies. Our enemies are fear, resentment, envy, mistrust, doubt, repressed anger, displaced anger, cowardice, discouragement, despair, lies and deceit.

Come the morning, all is well. God is with us. Out goes fear, doubt and mistrust. Anger, despair and discouragement are dissipated. God is with us. All is well. Today is the only day we have to live and live well. If this was the last day of your life, how would you live it? You would live it fully, completely, intensely, honestly and totally alive to everything and everybody.

"This is what knowledge really is. It is finding out something for oneself with pain, with joy, with exultancy, with labour, and with all the little ticking, breathing moments of our lives, until it is ours as that only is ours which is rooted in the structure of our lives."

THOMAS WOLFE

What is "rooted in the structure", of my life today? I am not sure. But I have learned one thing slowly and painfully; to face fear, to face each fear as it arrives, is the only way to defeat it.

I have also learned to deal with things as they are, to look things straight in the face and see them for what they are, not to run away to stand and face the enemy.

I have learned to keep my feet on the ground but my eye on the far horizon.

I have learned to be, to act and to use my body as it was intended.

I have learned to live fully in the present as much as possible, to more and more let go of all negative thinking, to laugh, to live, to walk, to run, to cycle, to stand and fight when needed, to turn away from all destructive forces and towards all creative ones.

I have learned to let go of the past and move forward bravely into the future.

"For one human being to love another: that is perhaps the most difficult of all our tasks, the ultimate, the last test and proof, the work for which all other work is but preparation."

RILKE MARIA RAINER

It is difficult to love another because first we must love ourselves. To love ourselves we need to fully accept ourselves; to accept all about us, all our past and every aspect of our being. To love ourselves, we need to know ourselves; to know the deepest recesses of our being. This is a lifelong job. It is a lifelong journey into our core. It is a journey that leads to self-knowledge, self-acceptance and self-forgiveness. We need to forgive ourselves for all our mistakes, all our wasted opportunities and wasted time, all our lack of self-love, all the damage done to ourselves and others. Let God be your partner on this journey as he is the only one that truly knows you. At the absolute centre of your being is pure love; for yourself, for others and for God your Creator.

"This, then, must be life's work. One task is completed and another is ready to my hand!"

LEO TOLSTOY

Life goes on until the end. We do not know when the end will come. Today is the day. It is the first day of the rest of my life. Whatever happened yesterday, today can be better. Today you can change your thinking, let go of all past resentments, jealousies, hurts and angers. Today you can clear out all the rubbish from your home and your mind. Today you can make a list of all the things you have not done and start doing number one. Today you can make a list of all the people you love and appreciate. You can take that list and start to thank the first person on that list for all they have done for you and been for you. Today you can make a list of all the things in your life and be grateful for them.

"JAZZ 111"

WEEK 13

"Give away time. Time is something there never seems to be enough of, hence it is one of our most valuable commodities. It is also one of our most precious gifts."

SUSAN JEFFERS

"Break some of your comfortable / boring routines. You will know what these are."

LYNDA FIELD

Routine is good in itself. It helps get you through the day and the week. It helps with self discipline. It gets routine maintenance tasks done on a regular basis. It helps with the smooth running of your life and work.

But it can also be a trap, a false support keeping you in a situation that is not good for you, stopping you from exploring the big wide world. There is a great deal of wonderful, amazing and good things in this world. Take a risk today. Do something different. Take a different route home. Plan an outing to a place you have never been before. Change your hairstyle. Write to a distant relative. Buy and wear a new tie. Visit a church or a graveyard. Surprise your family, your boss or your beloved in some way. Buy yourself some delightful little present.

"All this terrible change had come about simply because he had ceased to put his faith in his own conscience and had taken to trusting in others."

LEO TOLSTOY

Our conscience is our deep inner awareness of what is right for us or wrong for us. I believe it is God operating within us. God's voice is always gentle. We must listen very carefully for it. Whether or not you believe it, it is there deep within us. Some people call it their 'gut', or instinct or intuition. Whatever you call it, it exists. It is a gift we all have been given. It is deeper than our reasoning minds. Often our reasoning mind tells us one thing but our gut or intuition tells us another. Trust your gut. That is God talking or God prompting you in a certain direction or away from another direction.

Conscience is really consciousness of God within. Your conscience will always guide you to do what is right for you. Other people have their consciences to guide them. First things first, always put yourself in God's care first. Be willing to do God's will not your own, to allow God's plan to develop not your own.

"We're drowning in information and starving for knowledge."
RUTHERFORD   D   ROGERS

What is knowledge? It is understanding. It is knowing the truth of a situation. The more and more information that is collected and stored, the greater the confusion that ensues. Life becomes bewildering and complex. Everything slows down. Simplicity goes out the window and so does trust. We no longer trust our instincts, our judgment, our Creator. We trust processes and procedures which inevitably fail to meet their objectives. They let us down and cost a great deal in time, money and energy.

Keep it simple. Trust your own judgment. Stand back and have a look. Only by detaching and standing back can we see what is really happening. Clarity comes in time and with it understanding and true knowledge.

"There is a power of love that overcomes everything and that lives in the hearts of all human beings... It is a source of joy and freedom as it reveals to us our divine potential."

HARVEY GILLMAN

We all have a divine design on our lives. There are things that only we can do. There are things we were put on this earth to do. It comes as flashes of images; things that seem too good to be true; our true life, the life we were meant to be living. In order for the divine design of our lives to manifest we need first to surrender our lives and our wills to God our Creator. Stay close to God and wait to be shown the way. The guidance will come. The opportunities will come. Listen with your inner ear for the prompting of God. Go with your gut, your intuition or with 'a feeling'. Very often this is from God, from the God within pointing you in the right direction. Listen and act.

God is not the only one who prompts us. The tempter or the evil one is alive and well. How do you know which is which? By the results; God will always lead you to peace, joy, abundance, health, clarity and well being. The evil one's promptings lead to confusion, doubt, despair, despondency, degradation and rationalization.

"Yahweh, who can find a home in your tent, who can dwell on your holy mountain? Whoever... casts no discredit on a neighbour."

PSALMS 15:1 – 3

So who is my neighbour? Everybody we have contact with or dealings with. What does "to discredit" mean? I think it means to show people up in a bad light, to say negative things about them and to take their good name. To discredit someone is to take away their credit. So instead of giving them credit for all the good they do or are, to discredit is to take all that away, to negate it. So what are we being asked for here? I think we are being asked to focus on the positive aspects of our neighbour not the negative, not their wrong-doings. How can you do this? You can do this by praying for them especially when things are difficult. Keep on praying for them. The situation may get worse before it gets better. If action is needed guidance will come and difficulties will resolve themselves eventually.

"I buried, when I saw them, the bodies of my country-folk thrown over the walls of Nineveh. I also buried those who were killed by Sennacherib."

                                                    TOBIT 1:17 – 18

   Tobit got into a lot of trouble for burying the dead. Respect for the dead is very important, both for their remains and their spirits. Whether or not we have been able to bury all the members of our family tree, we can still bless their remains and the place or places their remains reside in or have resided in. We can do this at a distance even if we do not know where they are. God knows, and if we ask him to bless their remains and place or places they reside in, he will. Our family tree is all of our living and dead blood relatives and their spouses and any one they had children with. It is necessary to go back seven generations when praying for our family trees. Somewhere in the Bible it states that we can be affected by the sins of our ancestors back seven generations.

"SOUTH MALL"

WEEK 14

"But now a new history commences: a story of the gradual renewing of a man, of his slow progressive regeneration, and change from one world to another – an introduction to the hitherto unknown realities of life."

FYODOR DOSTOYEVSKY

"Grant to me that I may be made beautiful in my soul within...
May I consider the wise man rich."

SOCRATES

This is so totally against the modern ideas, where it is
the external that matters: your physical appearance, clothes,
hairstyle, teeth, your car, your address or your connections.
Who nowadays strives to "be made beautiful in my soul
within"? What is a beautiful soul? How would you know if you
had one? It is said that the eyes are the mirrors of the soul.
Peace and joy shows in a person's eyes as a light shining. Soul
death shows itself as a darkness or deadness around the eyes.

Do I "consider the wise man rich"? I do not know. How
can I identify a wise man or woman? Wisdom and serenity go
together I think, so I would look for serenity and I would look
for joy. Joy and a great sense of humour comes with wisdom.
Wise men and women have learned to live well and grow where
they are planted.

They have learned to enjoy all the good there is in life.
They have learned to challenge, let go of or avoid the bad there
is in life. They have learned or continue to learn to differentiate
between the things to stand firm on and the things to let go of.
Wisdom comes from being able to deal with life as it is. So are
"wise men rich"? Yes, very definitely.

"May I have such wealth as only the self-restrained man can bear or endure."

SOCRATES

This goes against the modern grain which advocates more, more, more: more money, more houses, more goods, more cars, more sex, more drink, more holidays. The idea that wealth must be 'endured' is strange to us. But with wealth comes responsibility, the responsibility to use wisely, to maintain and secure it. All sorts of insurances and security matters come into play with wealth. There is also the situation of avoiding being conned or charmed or sued out of your wealth. There is also the responsibility of deciding whether a person likes you for yourself or your money. A wealthy person has the responsibility to dispose of their wealth after they die.

I think Socrates is also getting at the idea of simplicity. The simpler you keep your life the easier it is. The fewer possessions you have the less responsibility you have. Possessions can tie you down.

It is good to do a thorough clear out of your possessions. I once had to reduce all my family's possessions down to one cubic meter of goods, the contents of four large suitcases and four small backpacks. It was a painful but freeing experience. I learned what possessions were important and which ones I could live without.

"Someone once described the act of hating and resenting as being like 'hugging a poisonous snake to our bosom'. Feelings of ill will fester and eventually erupt, often making us ill."

LYNDA FIELD

Letting go of hatred and resentment is a huge thing. It is a gigantic step forward in your personal and spiritual life. You first need to make a list of all the people you hate, resent or just plain dislike. Start with the easiest the person you least dislike and pray for him or her. Pray for them and bless them. Every time that person comes into your mind pray for them and bless them. Keep on doing it until all resentment goes fully. Then go to the next person on the list until it is completely cleared. Once you start praying for a person on the list, anger may emerge. Let it come, write down how you feel. Let all the anger out unto the page. Keep on writing until all the anger is spent. Keep on praying for them. Things will happen. You will change. They will change. Keep it up, it really is worth it. All is well. All is well.

"Think Love, and Love surrounds you. Think thoughts of ill will, and ill surrounds you, and all those about whom you think. Think health – health comes. The physical reflects the mental and spiritual."

TWO LISTENERS

This is true. What we think and say is so important. We need to keep our minds on positive, life-affirming things all the time.

Think love: love yourself, love your neighbour, love all you come in contact with, love all you deal with everyday, love all you are related to, love all in the country you live in, love all in the whole world. A tall order. Start with yourself. Think loving thoughts about yourself. What do you like about yourself? What are you proud of about yourself? What have you accomplished in life so far? Lots, you have lived until today. Every day lived is a victory. Have you brought any children into this world? To have given birth or fathered another human being is a huge achievement. Well done. Keep on thinking about all the good you are or have done. Keep writing it down.

"Perfect yourself on this man, give him a perfect, unselfish love, demanding nothing in return, do not criticize or condemn and bless him wherever he is."

FLORENCE SCOVEL SHINN

This is an awful lot to ask of someone; to give "a perfect unselfish love, demanding nothing in return". We so much want to be loved in return or to have people the way we want them to be. We want to fashion others to our own design. So many relationships are based on the unwritten contract – I'll be good to you, if you behave in such and such a way. I'll love you if you give me what I want in return.

"Do not criticize or condemn". This takes a lot of effort and practice. It is not just the verbalized criticisms that count alone but also the mental ones. Condemning someone in your mind is so easy. To stop it, you need first to be aware of it, then you must say no to your mind and replace the condemning though with a positive, blessing one. To keep on blessing someone, even though you are angry with them, is difficult, but rewarding.

Pick one person today not to criticize or condemn. Bless that person all day long and amazing things will happen to you.

110

"'Why has my Lord the King come to his servant?' Araunah asked. David replied, 'to buy the threshing-floor from you, to build an alter to Yahweh, so that the plague may be lifted from the people.'"

2 SAMUEL 24:21

Servant. What is a servant? One who serves. One who obeys. Whom do we serve? Whom do we obey? Do we bow down at the altar of people-pleasing? Do we serve our country or our company or our family or ourselves alone? Do we bow down at the altar of fashion, beauty, fitness, intellect or caring for others? Do we obey the dictates of the media, the group, our parents or a religious sect or denomination? Is the attainment of material wealth and possessions our primary life aim or is love and relationships or children or fun or fame? What is the main purpose or driving force in our lives? What do we give the most attention to in our daily lives? What is the most important thing in our lives?

Could this be our plague, our individual plague? Perhaps it is an obsession or compulsion or an addiction that we need to be freed from. Who can free us from this? Only God our Creator and only by our surrender to him.

"FITZGERALD PARK"

WEEK 15

"Freedom of conscience and the free profession and practice of religion are, subject to public order and morality, guaranteed to every citizen."

CONSTITUTION OF IRELAND,
ARTICLE 44:2.1

"You are unique. There is no such thing as a normal or average size or type of person. Everyone is absolutely special and individual."

LYNDA FIELD

Yes, you are unique. There is no one like you. Every cell in your body is special, not like anyone else's. Even identical twins have different fingerprints and spirits. There never was anyone else like you and there never will be again. The reason for your existence is special too. There is some thing or more than one thing that only you can do and no one else. They may not be the things that generate fame and fortune or even get you noticed, but they are there. The purpose of our lives is spiritual. We are here to improve our own and others' spiritual lives. It is in working out our own salvation that we inadvertently help others, often in ways we are not aware of. All true failures are spiritual ones: failure to let God help us, to surrender ourselves, our children, our partners, our jobs, our country, to the care of God our Creator.

"Learn to make the very best use of your time; it is your most valuable resource."

LYNDA FIELD

Yes, it is. We do not know how much time we have. We do not know the day or the hour that our life on earth will end. Live every moment, every day as if it were your last. What do you need to do before dying? Do it today. Who do you need to see? What do you need to say to them? Is there anyone you need to make amends to? Is there anyone you need to say I love you to? Do it today. At least make a start today, plan it today. Have you made a will? Do your relatives know where it is? Do you have a grave or a plot for your remains? If you can, get one. Make the most of every day. Life is a gift from God. Live well. Live abundantly.

"Because we are mortal, every talent, skill, ability we possess, every thought and feeling we ever have, every beautiful sight we ever see, every material possession we own, will ultimately be lost. Unless we share it, unless we give what we have to others."

EDITORS OF CONARI PRESS

Give away. Yes, everything we give away comes back to us, not the exact same thing but similar and in great abundance. If we give away love and kindness love comes back to us from someone else. If we give away money or material possessions others come back to us in abundance. The more generous you are to life the more generous life is to you.

Everything you share increases. Every negative thing shared increases it, spreads it further – gossip, lies, fears, violence, deceit. Every positive thing shared increases it – love, kindness, generosity, goodness, joy and peace.

A trouble shared can be decreased provided that the person hearing it does not take on the fears of the other.
Everything has a ripple effect. It takes a lot of strength and power to stop the negative effect. This power can only come from God. Ask for it in your life.

"'The Philistines are on you, Samson!' He woke from his sleep and pulled out both reed and warp. So the secret of his strength remained unknown."

JUDGES 16:14

So what is the secret of your strength? Some people live on self will alone. This can get you a long way, but you can wear yourself out trying to force solutions. You may get what you want, but it may not be good for you.

Some people live on the will of others, others they admire, others they fear, others they believe are an authority and know better then them.

You can surrender your life and your will into the care of God your Creator. Take a risk. If your life is a mess you have nothing to lose. Surrender, one minute, one hour, one day. See if it makes a difference. God is with us. God will help us, if we let him.

"Nothing stands between man and his highest ideals and every righteous desire of his heart, but doubt and fear. When man can 'wish without worrying', every desire will be instantly fulfilled."

FLORENCE SCOVEL SHINN

So what do you wish for? If your fairy godmother was standing in front of you with her magic wand ready to grant you three wishes what would they be? What are the dearest wishes of your heart? Write them down. Ask God, the Creator to grant them. No fear. No doubt, just leave them with him.

Banish all fear. Replace it with faith and confidence. 'God is with me. I am safe. All is well. Good things are happening all the time. All my loved ones are safe. I am well. God is good. I am good.' These affirmations can be used to banish fear and doubt. Pick whichever one appeals to you most and say it over and over again.

"Follow the path of love, and all things are added, for God is love, and God is supply; follow the path of selfishness and greed, and the supply vanishes, as man is separated from it."

                                        FLORENCE SCOVEL SHINN

Do I really believe this? I am not sure. In the past I thought I was following the 'path of love'. Some good things came of it but also poverty, abuse and disease. But maybe I was following a path of attraction and desire, not true love. Maybe I did not truly love myself or maybe my love was conditional? I will love you if you give me all my heart's desires! It is too much to expect of anybody. True love accepts people the way they are, just the way they are for today. Whatever that may be and it does not try to control or mould another adult.

Do I believe that 'God is love'? Yes. Yes I do. God is love. Love comes from God and goes back to God. Being in love is a magical time and in some strange way it allows you to see the beloved as God intended, the perfect idea God has for that person. Of course in time you fall out of love and the vision fades. Can you then accept the person warts and all? Is this person good for you and to you? Maybe, maybe not, you will know the answer in time.

"SEAT"

WEEK 16

"He strode down the shady steps to the lodge-gate in a strange mood of rejoicing, realizing that however the city might change, that old love-affair went on unbroken in a world where disgust or despair would never touch it, and would continue to do so till both of them were dead."

FRANK O'CONNOR

"Do not waste time bothering whether you 'love your neighbour'; act as if you did. As soon as we do this we find one of the great secrets. When you are behaving as if you loved someone, you will presently come to love him."

C S LEWIS

Is this true? It is worth a try. What if you tried it for a day? Behave as if you love everyone you meet or have contact with today. That is everyone without exception. Banish all negative or critical thoughts, towards others from your mind, for one day. That is everyone, everyone you meet, everyone you talk to on the phone, everyone you contact through the post or e-mail or fax, everyone you see, everyone you think about. Act as if you love them. Act as if they are the most special person in the whole world. Act as if they are wonderful, precious and beloved above all. See how it goes. It is definitely worth a try.

"Let us come into his presence with thanksgiving; acclaim him with music."

PSALMS 95:2

The "him", referred to is God, in this case Yahweh. God is within us, all of us without exception.

"Let us come into his presence with thanksgiving." To come into God's presence within yourself, start with a gratitude list. List all the things you are grateful for. You are alive. Life is a gift. Every moment is a gift. Every moment up until this moment has been a gift. Every moment is precious, and once given can never be taken away. Every child you are the parent of is a gift, no matter how short or how long their life on earth is. Some children only live for a day. Once conception has occurred, life begins and you are a parent. Your spiritual condition affects your children and your children's children right down to seven generations. When you have your list completed thank God and praise God for everything and everybody on your list. Thank God and praise God for every moment of your life from the moment of your conception to this moment. Ask God to dissolve and dissipate all the effects of sin by and on your ancestors.

"Yahweh, God of my salvation, when I cry out to you in the night, may my prayer reach your presence, hear my cry for help."

PSALMS 88:1 – 2

"When I cry out to you in the night." Why is it that the night is such a difficult time? What is it that brings out all the demons at night, the demons of fear, doubt, lust, greed, self indulgence of every kind, anger, violence and hatred? Could it be the absence of light, sunlight and spiritual light? Certain orders of monks believe that prayer during the night is the most powerful kind of prayer. They believe that the devil rules at night because there are so few people awake and praying. So they get up and pray for us as we sleep. Once I got up at night specifically to pray for a person in great distress. There was an incredible feeling of stillness and power during the prayer session. Within a short space of time, the person I prayed for had started to fight back. He never knew that I prayed for him. Maybe other people have gotten up in the middle of the night and prayed for me. Who knows? We may never know in this life the number of people who have prayed for us and wished us well.

I remember one night driving to visit some body I knew in a mental hospital. I had been visiting this home maybe once or twice a year for the previous ten years. Those were ten of the most difficult years of my life. As I was driving along I knew with an absolute certainty that a lot of people from that mental home had held me in their prayers all those years.

"Blessed are those who observe his instructions, who seek him with all their hearts, and doing no evil, who walk in his ways."

PSALM 119:2 – 3

"His instructions" are God's instructions, his personal instructions to us, his is leadings, his guidance for our own lives.

"Seek him with all their hearts." That is, look inside yourself, into your own heart. What is your heart telling you today? Deep in your heart you know what is right. What is right for you in any given situation, at any given time?

When you walk in his ways you cannot do evil. Evil is everything that is destructive, destructive of life, of well-being, of spirit, of mind and of body. All the destructive forces in the world and in us are not from God or of God. God is goodness, creativity, life itself.

Murder is an enormous sin. To kill a human being is to say no to God, no to life. The consequences of murder are far reaching. It is a sin that can reverberate down though the generations, until both the murderer and the murder victim and their families have been prayed for and the effects have been neutralized.

"Blessed be Yahweh for ever. Amen, amen."

PSALMS 89:52

　　　　Yahweh is God. Yahweh is the name the Jewish people called God, the creator of heaven and earth. "Blessed be" God "for ever". It seems strange to bless God. To bless someone is to ask for good things for them. To be blessed is to be fortunate, to be bestowed with good health, or good fortune or both. Surly the blessings come from God and not to God. Perhaps it is a circular motion, we praise and thank God and he bestows blessings on us. The more we praise God and thank him, for all the good things he gives us, the more he delights in giving us good things. Start with gratitude and praise and end with abundance. Amen. Amen. So be it. So be it. Let it be done. Let it be done.

"Come, I beg you, look at me; man to man, I shall not lie."

JOB 6:28

"Look at me." See me for what I am. Turn your eyes on me. Put a mirror up to my soul. See into me. See me as I am. See all the pain and sorrow. See all the buried anger and deep pain. See all the good will and the ill will. See all the talents and capabilities. See all the memories and the effects of the past. See all the influences that shaped me. See what I was meant to be. See all the failures, the failures in love, the failures in surrender. See all. See all the possibilities good and bad.

"I shall not lie." Do we not all lie to ourselves? Keep ourselves hidden from ourselves. Hold up the mirror now. Behold yourself. Love yourselves.

"TOILET"

WEEK 17

"A journey of a thousand miles begins with the first step."

TAO

"Give thanks to Yahweh for he is good, for his faithful love endures for ever."

PSALMS 136:1

"Give thanks" now and for evermore. Give thanks every day for your life, no matter how bad things may appear to be for you. Life is a gift. Give thanks for it. Give thanks in every situation no matter how grim. Give thanks for every red light, every lost comb, every traffic ticket and every nasty word spoken against you. Give thanks for every job lost, every train missed and every love lost. Give thanks and praise to God for everything and the right outcome will emerge in time.

"Faithful love." Faithful love is so precious, in all circumstances. God loves us in every circumstance. God loves us in all circumstances. His love never varies. It does not depend on us being good, on doing what we are told, on obeying the rules or on keeping on his right side. God's love for us is unconditional and it "endures for ever". It is a perfect love. We are called to love him back in a perfect way too, in all circumstances. Therein lies the challenge. Face the challenge.

"When the Jews heard that Nicanor was coming and that the foreigners were about to attack, they sprinkled dust over themselves and made supplication to him who had established his people forever and who never failed to support his own heritage by direct manifestations."

2 MACCABEES 14:15

When the Jews knew that they were under threat they called on their God whom they knew would help them.

God is with us and there for us when we let him. All we need to do is call on him and believe that he will help us. In time believing becomes knowing, if we do not believe or know then act as if we do. Act as if God is there for us and he will help us. Go forward bravely into the future. Ask God's help. Put the situation into God's care and move out. Go forward. Face the future bravely. Go forward unafraid. Attack all fear with the truth. 'God is with me. All is well. All is well.

"Saying to Yahweh, 'My refuge, my fortress, my God in whom I trust.'"

PSALMS 91:2

Yahweh is the name given to God by the Jewish people. Trust in God your Creator, the Creator of heaven and earth. "My refuge", my safe haven, "My fortress", a fortress is a place of protection, a place where your enemies can not get at you. "My God", everyone was created by God with the assistance of their biological parents. Everyone has their own relationship with their Creator. Some people believe in existence only. They believe only in what they perceive with their senses. Others believe that there is one God, the Creator of heaven and earth and all living things.

What do you believe? Do you believe your Creator loves you and cares for you or hates you and wants to punish you? I believe that God loves me and cares for me no matter what. I can see this when I trust him. The more I trust him the greater the chance he has of working in my life and showing me his love for me. The more I surrender to him the more he can use me for his kingdom.

"The lover of Wisdom makes his father glad, but the patron of prostitutes fritters his wealth away."

PROVERBS 29:3

Those who spend money on prostitutes waste away their wealth. How many other things do we fritter away our wealth on? Borrowed money is one. All borrowed money is repaid with interest and additional charges. Today many people have credit cards, shop cards, personal loans and mortgage loan debt. Day by day they are storing up debt for the future. This is not good. A financial debt is a burden, a burden you do not need to carry. To be debt free is a great achievement and a state greatly to be desired and maintained.

How are we spending the money we do have? Do we fritter it away on junk of one kind or another: cigarettes, alcohol, unnecessary prescription drugs, sugar-based foods, junk food, eating out, expensive forms of transportation, excessive amounts of clothes, CDs, electronic devices? How much money do you need to have a good life, with all your bases covered and some for the future as a prudent reserve? A prudent reserve is a cushion of money for unforeseen circumstances, three months' living expenses is a good rule of thumb. Are you spending money on all of your necessities? Are you leaving yourself short in any area? Do you have money for fun? Do you spend money on small self-indulgences, which do not cost a lot but make you feel rich, like some strawberries or a flower for your button-hole?

"You, you alone, strike terror! Who can hold his ground in your presence when your anger strikes?"

PSALMS 76:7

The 'you' referred to here is Yahweh, the name given to God by the Chosen People.

There is a righteous anger, a healthy anger. An anger that is absolutely justified and correct. This anger no one can stand against. Healthy anger is not buried anger. It is rises immediately to the surface. It happens when a boundary is crossed, on yourself or someone you are connected to, or when your right to a decent life is threatened or shattered. With anger comes a huge amount of energy. This energy is made available to deal immediately with the situation. It is a tremendous 'No' from deep inside saying 'this is not right', 'this cannot be', 'what you are doing is wrong'. The energy is released to fight or flight. Both are natural and good responses. This anger needs to be released. It needs to be acted upon. Buried anger causes a great deal of illness. Overflowing flash anger causes a lot of damage to other people. Healthy anger is good. It points the way. It acts as a barometer of rightness. Hand it over to God your Creator. It will then be used for positive action, immediate action.

"Success, supply, harmony... these are but the outward manifestations that result from obedience, honesty, order, love – and they come, not in answer to urgent prayer, but naturally as light results from a lighted candle."

TWO LISTENERS

In other words, things work well in your life when you are right inside yourself. The world is not wrong, it is us who are out of harmony within ourselves. We are out of harmony with the God within. "Success, supply, harmony", these are the things we want in our lives. According to this quote, they spring from "obedience, order, love". The obedience referred to here is obedience to God's will for us, individually. That is, doing what God wants us to do in our own lives and in all the situations we face. In order to obey God's will for us, we must first of all surrender our will to God. Initially we need to do this as a lifelong commitment. Thereafter on a daily basis or an hourly or moment by moment basis as needed.

In order to know God's will for us, we need to listen to his promptings. His promptings are so gentle, we need to listen with the inner ear of our souls. Sometimes it is the chance word of a stranger or a word that keeps coming up, that guides us. God prompts very gently and quietly. It could be an ill ease about something, something undone or something we are doing that tells us this is wrong for us. Train your inner ear to listen to these promptings. Then obey immediately. Pray for guidance. Be willing to obey even the smallest prompt and marvellous things will happen. Amazing things will happen to you and others when you are on a spiritual path.

"CASTLE"

WEEK 18

"Love is an ideal thing, marriage is a real thing; a confusion of the real with the ideal never goes unpunished."

J W VAN GOETHE

"Never judge. The heart of man is so delicate, so complex, only its Maker can know it. Each heart is so different, actuated by different motives, controlled by different circumstances, influenced by different sufferings."

TWO LISTENERS

"Never judge." Never judge either another person's motives or the state of their soul. We just do not know. We can have insights into another person's soul to the degree that we understand ourselves and they mirror us. Some times we are given a glimpse into another soul as a grace from God. This is given for the benefit of ourselves or the other person. It is always given in love for love.

It is not our business to judge others' motives. However we do need to make good judgments for ourselves. Is it right to take this job? Is this person right for me to be friends with? Is this the right person for me to marry? These are important questions and we will be shown the right answers, for ourselves, in the situation, in time. The only person we need to continually judge is ourselves. What am I doing here? What do I need to change in myself? Do I need to do something about my health, my relationships, my accommodation, my appearance or my finances? What am I reacting too? Is she or he having a good effect on me? Am I going in the right direction? Keeping yourself in order mentally, physically, spiritually and financially is a full-time job. If you keep the focus on yourself, you will have no time to judge, condemn or criticize others.

"Satan, being thus confined to a vagabond, wandering, unsettled condition, is without any certain abode."

DANIEL DEFOE

I do not know a great deal about Satan. Part of me does not want to know, as whatever you concentrate on increases. But I do know that evil exists. It exists both within people and outside of people. I do not have any personal experience of hell in the after life. Some Christian saints have written accounts of being transported to hell during intense spiritual experiences. I read one such account by Saint Theresa of Avilla.

I do know people can live a hell of their own here on earth. Hell on earth is the total absence of God in your life. It is the total absence of guidance, of light, of hope, of love, of clarity, of direction, of certainty or of security within yourself. It is when this state becomes fixed for any length of time, that a person lives in a hell, often of their own making. In this life, there is a key to the door of our own hell. It is in our own hands. God exists. He does not leave us, we turn from him. Religion is good, if it acts as a bridge between God and us. Established religions have their place so long as they do not take the place of God. It is good to have a Sabbath day. It is good to have a routine of prayer and meditation and retreats from the world. It is good to formally place marriages, newborn babies and deaths in God's gentle hands.

"Unload your burden onto Yahweh and he will sustain you; never will he allow the upright to stumble."

PSALMS 55:22

Who are the upright? Everyone, who puts themselves into God's care. Yahweh is God. "Unload your burden", or cast your burden or throw your burden, "onto Yahweh". Your burden is all that troubles you, all that holds you back from having a full, abundant and joyous life. Your burden is all adverse conditions in yourself or your life. These adverse conditions are a reflection of inner ill ease or lack of harmony. All negative thinking, all repressed feelings, all destructive patterns of behaviour, all compulsions, obsessions and addictions, these are the burdens we bear. Cast these onto God. Give them all to God, to dissolve and dissipate. Once we have handed them over or cast the burden, we can relax. Keep our inner ear open for directions and we will be shown the way. Once we get guidance, act on it and things will work out in a marvellous way.

"Yes, you will go out with joy and be led away in safety. Mountains and hills will break into joyful cries before you and all the trees of the countryside clap their hands."

ISAIAH 55:12

The joy comes after a lot of suffering. I do not believe that God wants us to suffer. But we suffer for our own mistakes and we suffer for the mistakes of our ancestors. We are affected by the sins of our ancestors back seven generations and on both sides of our family tree. That is to say on our natural mother's side and our natural father's side. Every murder committed by any member of our family tree, or on them, every act of satanic worship, every curse made by them or on them, affects us. The only way to, neutralize and dissipate the effects of these sins are, to pray them away. Pray for your ancestors and pray for all these negative effects to be dissolved and dissipated.

The physical remains of our ancestors needs to be treated with respect. If we do not know where they are and cannot take care or them ourselves, then we can pray that the remains themselves and the ground they are in, be blessed. All known and unknown children conceived by ourselves and the members of our family tree, are included in our family tree. This covers all aborted, miscarried or stillborn babies. They also need our prayers and their remains needs to be treated with respect.

"'God preserve me', he said, 'from doing such a thing!'"
1 CHRONICLES 11:19

"God preserve me". God protect me,
God keep me from wrong doing,
God keep me from doing anything that would injure myself or others,
God keep me from going down a wrong path for me,
God keep me from marrying the wrong person,
God keep me from taking the wrong job,
God keep me from walking into danger,
God keep all those I hold in my heart, from all harm,
God keep me young in mind, body and spirit.

"As you receive, you must supply the needs of those I bring to you. Not questioning, not limiting, their nearness to you, their relationship, must never count. Only their need is to guide you. Pray to become great givers."

TWO LISTENERS

"Pray to become great givers." Give of your time, a most precious commodity. Give of your self, your attention, your talents, your perceptions. Give from your excess. Do not leave yourself short. Take care of yourself first. Give from what is left over and more will come to replace it. Give of your heart, give of your knowledge, give generously of your prayers. In prayer you place the other person or people in God's care. You can hand them over and let them go. Give of your senses. Give of your body, where appropriate. Never compromise your dignity, your integrity or your respect for yourself. Give small things and big things. Let God be your guide and the need of the other person. Give whatever the other person needs not what they want. "Pray to become great givers."

"HARBOUR"

WEEK 19

"The wise fears evil and avoids it,
the fool is insolent and conceited."

PROVERBS 14:16

"Using praise is one of the most powerful ways of allowing a child to feel good about herself."

LYNDA FIELD

Praise is good. Praise yourself. Praise yourself every time you do well. Praise yourself now for opening yourself up for this positive input. Praise yourself for every good and positive thing you have ever done. Praise your friends; praise your boss; praise your family for every good you can think of, whatever good they have done for you. Praise your neighbour. Praise your country. Praise God. The Bible repeatedly asks us to praise and thank God. Praise God for everything, first those things which appear good then those things which appear difficult, challenging or even tragic. Praise God no matter what you feel. Praise God for feeling the way you do, no matter how awful that may be. Praise God in all circumstances. Praise God for everything and miracles will happen.

"Look for beauty and joy in the world around. Look at a flower until its beauty becomes part of your very soul. It will be given back to the world again by you in the form of a smile or a loving word or a kind thought or a prayer."

TWO LISTENERS

"Look for beauty and joy in the world." This can be difficult, sometimes there can be so many distractions. There is beauty and joy in the world. It takes an effort to focus on it. You need to slow down to notice it. You need to stop obsessive thinking. You need to come into the present, take your head out of the past or the future. It takes an effort to turn away form all the ugliness and sorrow. But the effort is worth it. Right now look around you. What beauty can you see? Keep looking and you will find it: a piece of fruit, a flower, a child's face, your hands. It is there, look for it.

Focus on the positive, the good and the beautiful and it will grow. Whatever you pay attention to grows. Look for one flower in a dung heap and you will find more. Look for the good in people and it will increase. Say no to the negative and the beauty will increase, joy will emerge. The sunshine of life will burst out all over, you, your friends, your loved ones and over the whole world.

"Meat is to sustain the body. To do the will of God is the very strength and support of Life. Feed in that food."

TWO LISTENERS

"To do the will of God" you must first of all be willing. In order to be willing you need to surrender your life and your will to God. If you have not done it do it now. "I surrender my life and my will to you Lord now and for evermore." Now you need to do this every day for the rest of your life and in every situation you encounter and with every aspect of your being.

Once you are in God's care and willing to do his will, life will never be the same again. If you go down a path that is for you, it will either be blocked or you will suffer greatly for it. Sometimes the way forward is clear. Other times you just have to take a risk and see what happens. If it is right for you it becomes apparent and things will work out in time. If you ask for a definite lead you will be shown. A lead often comes by the same word cropping up again and again. God does talk to us, more in a whisper than a roar. So listen, tune your inner ear to his quiet voice and gentle leadings. If you have missed some leadings, apologize and start over again. Listen and obey.

"The quiet gray days are the days for duty."

TWO LISTENERS

Duty is what you are responsible for, what you are bound to do. It is a parent's duty to take care of their children or have someone else do it for them. It is your duty to take care of yourself once you reach adulthood. It is your duty to your boss or employer to do the job you are paid to do to the best of your ability. It is your duty with everyone you encounter to pray for them and treat them with respect. It is your duty to your community and your country to do what is right for them, within your capabilities. It is your duty to your home to keep it clean, comfortable and as pleasant as possible. It is your duty as a human being to get to know, love and serve God. May your love and understanding grow every day.

"It is the Law of grace, or forgiveness. It is the law which frees man from the law of cause and effect – the law of consequence.' Under grace and nor under law.'"

FLORENCE SCOVEL SHINN

Grace is a free gift from God, an unmerited favor, a direct divine intervention. We can ask for grace for ourselves or others.

The biggest grace of all is forgiveness. Ask God to forgive us our wrong doings, wrong thoughts, our mistakes, our omissions, all that we failed to do and all that we did that was not in accordance with his will for us. Ask God to heal the effects of the wrongs done by us. Now ask God to heal the effects of all the wrongs done to us. Once this is done we are free to let go of all resentment and buried anger towards others for their real or imagined slights towards us. Forgiveness is healing. Forgiveness comes at the end of the healing process. In the end there is nothing to forgive. All damage has been repaired. All lessons learned. Growth has happened. Love triumphs over all. Today is a new day. Start from today, bless everything that happens, bless everybody you meet or have contact with, bless every situation you are in. All is well. All is well.

"Then Raguel blessed the God of heaven with these words:
'You are blessed, my God, with every blessing that is pure; may
you be blessed for evermore!'"

TOBIT 8:15

To bless someone is to wish them well. To curse
someone is to wish them ill. All curses and blessings act as
boomerangs. It either comes back upon us or our descendents.
All ill will boomerangs back upon us or our descendents. It can
only be neutralized by the grace of God. We need to ask God to
forgive us for all the times we cursed ourselves, other people, or
groups of people or countries. We need to ask God to forgive
our ancestors for all the curses they made and to neutralize all
the curses made by them and on them. Start to bless everybody
you know now. That is everybody you have met, had contact
with or even thought about. Wish them well. Start with the
people you like and care about and move on to the people you
do not like, then move on to the people you feel anger and
resentment towards or positively hate. These are the challenging
ones and the most important ones for your own freedom. Make
a list. Keep working on it. Great rewards are in store for you.
Keep it up. Freedom is on the way.

"LAMP"

WEEK 20

"This is what I really feel in the inmost recesses of my soul. In this feeling, as we may call it, I cannot be mistaken because it can come from no one but God. He alone can penetrate the inner sanctuary of the soul and communicate with it directly. Into this deepest part of the soul no one has the power to enter except God."

PADRE PIO OF PIETRELCINA

"There is for each man, a perfect self-expression."
FLORENCE SCOVEL SHINN

Your "self-expression" is your unique set of abilities. It is something that you are really good at, something, a role that only you can play. There is a perfect plan in God's mind for all of us. It may not be anything dramatic, or anything that will lead to fame, but there is a place that we alone can fill and it is waiting for us. We can ask for the divine design of our life to be made manifest. We can ask to be shown the way. It will come to us as something too good to be true. When the opportunity comes, go for it. Do not hesitate. Hold the dream. It is your destiny and it will come true if you let it. No matter how difficult it is to obtain for other people, it will unfold easily for you. Go with it. Do not hesitate. Do not doubt. Go forward fearlessly into the future, your future. God is with you every step of the way. Do not worry if nothing seems to be happening. God is on the case. Rest and take care of yourself. Keep yourself spiritually well and fit. Do the ordinary things of life well. Dress well. Tidy up your affairs. Clean out your drawers, your presses and your house. Keep yourself in good condition physically, spiritually, mentally and financially. All is well. All is well.

"The step of a fool goes straight into a house, but a person of much experience makes a respectful approach."

ECCLESIASTICUS 21:22

I think this is saying, "look before you leap". Be alert and aware of your surroundings. Take in what is going on around you. Do not barge in on people or situations. Be alert at all times. Be alert to all the signals both from within and without. The inward signals come from God, or the God within. Trust your gut. If you get a strong signal not to go someplace, obey it. Keep your eyes and ears open at all times. Look, listen, learn. Expect the unexpected. Be open-minded. Trouble always shows signs of approaching. Read the signs and act on it. Be alert. God is with you. Let him work. Let him take care of you. Let him show you the way, to safety, to prosperity, to health, to healing and to love.

"Regret nothing. Not even the sins and failures. When a man views earth's wonders from some mountain height he does not spend his time in dwelling on the stones and stumbles, the faints and failures, that mark his upward path. So with you. Breath in the rich blessings of each new day – forget all that lies behind you."

TWO LISTENERS

"Regret nothing." Everything that happens can teach us a lesson; a lesson in living, a lesson in compassion, a lesson in foolishness. Everything that happens can be handed over to God our Creator. Put all the past, up until this moment, into God's gentle hands. Good will come of it. All the pain and suffering can be converted into good. All the mistakes, all the wrong-doing, can be converted into compassion for yourself and others. All the good and right things can be converted into joy. The negative effects of all the mistakes and wrong-doings can be dissolved and dissipated. If you are willing to see the truth and act upon it, amends can be made for wrong-doing. Today is the first day of the rest of your life. This day will only come once. Enjoy it. Look with wonder at what is before you. All is well. All is well.

"Claim big, really big things now. Remember nothing is too big. Satisfy the longing of My Heart to give. Blessing, abundant blessing, on you both now and always. Peace."

TWO LISTENERS

"Claim big, really big things now." Does he really mean it? Can we ask for anything we want? Yes. But to be prudent, we need to qualify it with a request that only if it is God's will and to come in a perfect way and at the perfect time.

One Christmas, myself and my children were walking past a lot of car outlets on the way to a party. I said X was the brand of car I would really like to own. Within six months I got the opportunity to buy one of these cars at a reasonable price. I bought the car and had many years of safe and happy driving in it. It was not until some years later that I remembered that walk and my Christmas wish. This year I asked for a Christmas wish. It was very specific and I qualified it with "or its equivalent". I did not get the speficly asked for but something far better.

I have in the past been conscious of what I asked for but did not get, yet. Sometimes the answer is no, or not yet. Maybe the answers came and I did not see them for what they were. I know that prayers for guidance are always answered when I relax and open my mind. Peace and joy always comes after releasing unexpressed feeling or working through a problem to its core.

So think big. Ask for the best, the perfect, only what is really good for you, and it shall be granted to you in the perfect time and the perfect way.

"Never yield one point that you have already won. Discipline, discipline. Love it and rejoice – rejoice. Mountains can be removed by thought – by desire."

TWO LISTENERS

"Never yield one point that you have already won." Do not doubt. Once you have guidance, act on it. Once you have clarity, hold the thought, write it down. Once you have a victory, rejoice, rejoice and move on. All victories are in truth over yourself, over some fear or inadequacy in yourself, some false idea or thought. Go forward, let go of the past. Wrap it up in a blanket and hand it into the gentle hands of God. Onward and upward, God is always with you, there to help if you let him. Leave all past successes and failures behind you. Any failures will come again in a different guise. This time around you will get closer to success, with God's help and guidance. Onwards and upwards, regret nothing. Everything that happens shapes you and prepares you for today's challenges. God is good. All his purposes are good. Every thought and action has an effect, you may not see it but it is there. The more you surrender to the divine, the more positive are your actions and thoughts. Keep on surrendering one day, one moment at a time. All is well. All is well.

"Life with me is not immunity from difficulties, but peace in difficulties. My guidance is often by shut doors. Love bars as well as opens."

TWO LISTENERS

Sometimes, you would get the impression from spiritual and religious sources, that if you are following 'the path' or doing 'the right thing' that life would be free from difficulties. That is not true. Troubles come and sometimes they seem to come more often and quicker to those who are on a spiritual path. God is teaching us. If we do not learn our lesson quickly and well, it will be repeated in another form over and over again until we get the message. So what is he trying to teach us? One of the biggest lessons is not to fear. Whoever said "there is nothing to fear but fear itself", was spot on. There is also the lesson of the shut doors. It means not now or not at all. It is a way that God talks to us, so listen. Listen and learn. Pay attention, be alert. Wake up.

"WALL"

WEEK 21

"Trust wholeheartedly in Yahweh,
put no faith in your own perception;
acknowledge him in every course you take,
and he will see your paths are smooth."

PROVERBS 3:5 – 6

"Here and I answer. Spend much time in prayer. Prayer is of many kinds, but
of whatever kind, prayer is the linking up of the soul and mind and heart to God."

TWO LISTENERS

"Soul and mind and heart", that is your spiritual self. Link up your spiritual self to God, heart to heart, mind to mind and soul to soul. The ideal is a complete linking up to God. To reach it, you must surrender. Surrender your heart to God and all that is in it; all the hurt, all the anger, all the pain, all your dreams and all your desires. In time your wounds will be healed, your anger dissipated, your pain worked through and all your dreams and wished granted. Write down the three dearest wishes of your heart. Put it away. Some day you will come across it and be surprised. You will have been granted them in ways that you never expected or they will have dissipated, vanished into thin air and been replaced by other wishes. All is well. All is well.

"Have no fear. A very beautiful future lies before you. Let it be a new life, a new existence, in which in every single happening, event, plan, you are conscious of Me."

TWO LISTENERS

The "me" referred to here is God. The two listeners were two women who got together to pray and listen to God. They wrote down what they believed God said to them. They were in very poor and difficult circumstances when they first met. Their circumstances did not improve for a very long time. Yet God keep telling them to trust and not to fear. So much of what is wrong in our lives is a reflection of inner turmoil, both emotional and mental. It is being in a state of dis- ease. The inside must change first, then the outside manifests the changes. The better you get on the inside, the better your life gets on the outside. Troubles still come but we deal with them quicker and more effectively. They do not completely overwhelm us or they do overwhelm us but for a shorter time. The great lesson in life is: God is with us, do not fear, no matter how things may appear on the outside. All is well. All is well, for those who surrender themselves and their loved ones to God.

"Only in relationship can you know yourself, not in abstraction, and certainly not in isolation."

J KRISHNAMURTI

Is this true? Other people do mirror us but, do we see what is in the mirror? Some relationships can be a big distraction. Other people can distract us from focusing on ourselves. However other people can certainly teach us a lot. Only if we step back and ask ourselves the question, what is happening here? Why am I reacting in such a way to such a person or situation? Relationships can become addictive and obsessional. This is not healthy. Obsessive wanting of anything is not good. Wanting some one, specific person not in your life at the moment to be in your life, wanting someone to behave in a certain way, wanting more of someone's company than they are willing to give, this is an addiction. We need to let go of all addictions and obsessions. This can only be accomplished by the grace of God, ask for grace on a daily or a moment by moment basis.

"When things are going well, enjoy yourself, and when they are going badly, consider this: God has designed the one no less then the other, so that we should take nothing for granted."

ECCLESIASTES 7:14

"When things are going well, enjoy yourself." Live in the present. Enjoy all the good of today. Make the best of today. Enjoy the best of where you are living. There is some good in every place you are and everybody you meet. Let all thoughts of worry and doubt go from your mind. Do you hear the birds singing? Are there children playing near by? Are there lovers walking hand in hand? Is the sun shining? Does the rain fall softly against the window pane? Are there flowers in bloom? Enjoy every little bit of goodness. Who knows what tomorrow will bring. Every moment of life is precious. None can be taken for granted. Are your children alive today? Thank God for every one of them and every moment of their lives so far. Is there one human being who cares about you? If so, rejoice and thank God, if not, God loves you and cares about every hair on your head. Believe it.

"Lose sight of all limitations. Abundance is God's supply. Turn out all limited thoughts. Receive showers and in your turn – shower."

TWO LISTENERS

"Abundance is God's supply." In nature the rule is abundance. All seeds are produced in great abundance. Only one sperm is needed for conception but millions can be produced at each ejaculation. When things are working well in nature there is wonderful abundance. When things go wrong they go terribly wrong, bringing drought, famine, floods and earthquakes. The grace of God is the difference. Everything comes in its season. Winter comes before spring, the darkness comes before the dawn. Prosperity often comes after a period of poverty and lack. First feel rich, banish all thoughts of lack from your consciousness. In time the riches will come.

Give out lots and lots will be given back to you. So shower all the good things. Give out love, time, compassion, fun, music and dancing. Give out food, money and clothing. Give out space, peace and joy. Give, give, give. Give a smile, a thought, a prayer. Give, give, give.

"Lo, I am with you always, even to the end of the world."
MATTHEW 28:20

The "I", referred to here is God, the God of creation, the God of love. When God is with us, who can be against us? No one. Once you put yourself into God's care everything that happens will be for your ultimate good. Keep asking God to take care of you and yours.

Trust that all is well no matter about the outward appearance of things. We may not see the effects of our situations or our actions now but God is working in our lives and things are being worked out for the best. Baptize every event a success. If you get a red light baptize it a success; if your house burns down baptize it a success; if someone you are close to dies, it is very painful but baptize it a success. All is well. All is well. All is well.

Once I had a little job taking care of an elderly neighbour. There came a time when I knew he was no longer able to take care of himself. At that time places in nursing homes were hard to get. One day I went over to him to discover him on the floor. He had had an accident, which led to him losing the use of his legs. Because of his condition he got a place in a nursing home, where he lived happily for another two years.

"SHIPS"

WEEK 22

"All is well. Wonderful things are happening. Do not limit God at all. He cares and he provides."

TWO LISTENERS

"Seek in every way to become child-like, seek, seek, seek until you find, until the years have added to your nature that of a trusting child. Not only for its simple trust must you copy the child-spirit, but for its joy in life, its ready laughter, its lack of criticism, its desire to share all with all men."

TWO LISTENERS

Simplicity, clear sightedness, the ability to live in the present, to feel and express feelings on the spot, to be able to get to the heart of the matter, these are child-like qualities. Young children have no guile, no plan, no plot, no strategy. This is how God wants us to live, open only to his guidance, his prompting, seeing only with his eyes into the heart of the matter or the heart of the person we are dealing with. Simplicity is God's plan. Trust him to guide you to the best place for you to be. Perfect supply, perfect happiness, perfect health and perfect self-expression, these are his will for us, here and now in this world. Trust is the most important thing. Trust and let go. Let go of all fear, all doubt and all negative thinking. You will be shown the way. You will be shown the truth. Trust and wait. Wait for guidance before you act. Sometimes you need to act and see what happens. If it is wrong it will become apparent. Trust and wait or trust and act. All will work out. All will be revealed.

"She went and made the bed in this room as he had ordered, and took her daughter to it. She wept over her, then wiped away her tears and said, 'Courage daughter! May the Lord of heaven turn your grief to joy! Courage daughter!' and she went out."

TOBIT 7:16

"Courage is fear that's said its prayers" (source unknown). Courage is needed to live. It takes courage to get up in the morning. It takes courage to face the day. It takes courage to leave the house. It takes courage to face the world.

"She wept", weeping, crying and sobbing are all good. It is good to feel your sadness and loss. It is only through weeping and sobbing that we can release our hurt, our grief. Deep hurt and pain left inside will fester and turn into physical illness or mental and emotional ill ease.

"May the Lord of heaven turn your grief to joy!" Expressed grief turns into joy. Expressed grief, releases all pain and hurt, heals the wounds caused by loss, shock, violence and ill will. When the hurt has been released, drained and healed, joy is our natural state. When small children are given what they need and are not in any pain, they are joyful, ever ready to smile or laugh. Smile and laugh. Smiling keeps seriousness at bay. Laughter keeps illness at bay. Smile and laugh much, today and everyday.

"The whole assembly agreed to this, because all the people thought this was the right thing to do."

CHRONICLES 13:4

In this section of the Bible, David, who was King, first asked God to guide him. He then talked to all the commanders. After that he put the matter to the whole assembly. The ultimate authority in this matter rested with David. We have authority over our own actions and over our reactions to others, irrespective of our circumstances. David put the matter in God's hands first. This we can do with all our affairs. Then he put it to all the leaders. We can research the matter and seek expert and not so expert opinions. When the whole assembly agreed he then went forward with the decision. He put it into action. The consensus David got was that, 'it was the right thing to do'. Once we have put the matter into God's hands and done our research, we finally we get a sense of what is the right thing to do. We can act, knowing that whatever the outcome God is with us and God will take care of it.

"He finds that fear and worry are deadly sins. They are inverted faith, and through distorted mental pictures, bring to pass the thing he fears. His work is to drive out their enemies (from the subconscious mind)."

FLORENCE SCOVEL SHINN

"Fear and worry are deadly sins." Yes, they are the enemy. They need to be rooted out at every opportunity. How do you root out fear? By replacing it with its opposite. The opposite of fear and worry is faith and trust. Believe that all is well. Say it to yourself: "all is well", over and over again. Say it out loud. Believe that once you surrender yourself and your cares to God, he is with you. Say "God is with me". Say it to yourself, over and over again. Say it out loud when possible. "All is well. God is with me." "Everything is working out for the best." "God is good, I am good."

You can also drive out fear by facing it. Go right up to the person or situation you are afraid of and it will melt away in front of you.

"A colored student once made this wonderful statement. 'When I asks the Father for anything. I puts my foot down, and I says: Father, I'll take nothing less than I've asked for, but more! So man should never compromise. ...... The temptation comes to give up, to turn back, to compromise."

FLORENCE SCOVEL SHINN

There is a huge temptation to give up when things do not seem to be happening, when all seems the same and no change has occurred. This is when you need other people to pray for you. You need at least one other person to pray for you at all times. Any prayer fellowship or group is good for this. You need spiritual backing, everyone does. There are monks and nuns who dedicate their lives to praying for others, ask them to pray for you and they will. Negativity arises from within and both attacks and attracts from without. Scovel Shinn believes it is all from within and the outward reflects this. I am not so sure. Certainly this is true but I think there is a separate and distinct power for evil, working against us all the time. It works within us and attacks us from outside as well. We need constant protection from this evil force. That is why prayer is so vital. We need to constantly hold ourselves and others in prayer. Pray for complete protection, pray for perfect love, pray for perfect health, pray for perfect supply and perfect self expression. Never tire in prayer. Prayer recreates.

"For thus said the Lord God, the Holy one of Israel;
'In returning and rest you shall be saved, in quietness and in trust shall be your strength.'"

ISAIAH 30:15

It is so difficult sometimes to rest, to stand still and wait to really trust in the Lord: to trust God. The tendency is to force solutions; to try to make things the way you want them to be, to decide what the 'right answer' is and to try to force that into being. We do not always know what the right answer is. Some times clarity comes and we are very sure but not always. So to bridge the gaps of our uncertainty, we need to trust. To trust that all is well, that nothing will pass us by if it is for us, that we will be shown the right direction for us in the right time. In the meantime what do we do? We continue to perform our duties and follow our routines and lead our normal life with regular prayer and meditation, exercise and good food.

Routine and normality wear away the rough spots of life. The daily carrying out of tasks is balm for the soul. Simplicity and routine wear away the doubts and level the heights. A simple task well done sooths the fevered brain. Sun up and sun down, life goes on. New life is born and old life expires. The grass grows and the grass dies and so the cycle of life goes on. Only love lasts forever. Everything done in love lasts for eternity.

"HABOUR"

WEEK 23

"I felt so damn happy, if you want to know the truth. I don't know why. It was just that she looked so damn nice, the way she kept going around and around, in her blue coat and all. God, I wish you could've been there."

J D SALINGER

"We've had enough of following our whims; it's time to be reasonable. And all this, all this life abroad, and this Europe of yours is all a fantasy, and all of us abroad are only a fantasy."

FYODOR DOSTOYEVSKY

Fantasy and reality. What is fantasy and what is reality? Is not reality how we view it and is that not our own interpretation of it and is that not a result of our world view, which is a result of our conditioning and experience? Is not our conditioning based on someone else's fantasy? Does not our fantasy of today become our reality of tomorrow? Yes. That makes our ability to fantasize very important. We need to hand over our fantasies and our fantasizing facility to God, to be used in a creative and positive way. Imagining or fantasizing death, disease or disaster is not good. We do not want these things to come into being, so do not fantasize about them. Do not expect the worst or you will get it. Think only good for yourself and others. Ask God to put the right pictures in your mind, about yourself, your future and others. There is a perfect self-expression for you. Ask God to give you a picture of this. Ask God to show you the way, one step at a time, to put you on the right path and to keep you on it.

"Man should always demand only that which is his by divine right."

FLORENCE SCOVEL SHINN

What is yours by divine right? That which is perfect for you, God knows what is right for you. He knows the perfect spouse for you, he knows which is the perfect home for you, the perfect job for you, the perfect friends for you. So let him choose them for you. Every day and at all times there is a right place for you to be at and right people for you to meet and have contact with. Ask for it, ask for it every day.

Lord, the Lord of my life, Creator of my being:
let everything that happens to me today be from your hand,
let everything I think, say and do today be completely in accordance with your will for me,
let me be open to all your prompts today,
and let me act on them immediately.
Amen.

"Many people, however, are in ignorance of their true destinies and are striving for things and situations which do not belong to them, and would only bring failure and dissatisfaction if attained."

FLORENCE SCOVEL SHINN

How do you know your true destiny? That indeed is the question. According to Scovel Shinn it flashes across your consciousness as something too good to be true, something unbelievably wonderful, amazing and fantastic. So, I suppose if you ask yourself, what is the most wonderful, fantastic thing that I could be doing? That would give you a clue to the answer. What is the situation you would most like to be in? That is it. Hold the dream. It is your destiny.

Ask God to help you bring into being your dream and he will, in time and in a perfect way.

"For if you act in truthfulness, you will be successful in all your actions, as everyone is who practices what is upright."

TOBIT 4:6

Is this right? Sometimes it seems that if "you act in truthfulness" you get a huge backlash of hatred, malice, envy and spite from other people. What is truthfulness? Is it being true to yourself? Is it being true to your beliefs? Is it standing back and asking why am I doing this?

Who nowadays "practices what is upright"? To be upright is to stand up for what is right, to be upstanding.

Once I walked away completely from a situation where I was being demeaned. I felt wonderful, upstanding and dignified. I had by my actions said no to being treated like dirt.

"But God gives joy generously when he so wishes, and sometimes allows us sorrow; and both come from love."

JULIAN OF NORWICH

Sorrow is part of life. It cannot be eradicated completely in this life. The thing is, to feel the sadness, mourn the dead and all the other losses of life. The sooner we feel the sadness the quicker the joy will return. Do not suppress the pain. Pain is part of life. It takes pain to be born, pain to grow, pain to feel the limits of our existence. Letting go is painful. It is painful to let go of friendship, to let go of love from any source, to let go of children as they grow up, to let go of loved ones as they die, to let go of specific dreams when they do not materialize, to let go of things as they get lost, stolen or burned. Letting go is painful but good. All old sorrows, deep emotional pain and woundedness needs to go, to be released. So let go of all resentment, all sorrow, all past expectations, all old loves. Let it all go and let the joy flood in. God is with you. So who can be against you? No one. "Joy cometh in the morning."

"All shall be well; the fullness of joy is to see God in everything."

JULIAN OF NORWICH

This is really, really difficult. "The fullness of joy", that is, complete and continuous joy, is to "see God in everything". To see God is to see God's hand, the action of God, the movement of God, the goodness of God. "To see God in everything" - can Julian be really serious? Perhaps it is that the potential is there for God to enter into every happening and good to come of it. We then need to trust that all is well, that God is taking care of us. Praise God for everything that happens. Bless everything that happens. Accept, accept and hand over to God everything that happens. Then the negative effects are stopped and God enters in to make all things new again. Indeed better than ever.

To keep on believing that all shall be well, no matter what the present appearance of the situation, is difficult, but worth it. To keep on praising God no matter what is difficult, but not impossible. Keep it up.

All shall be well.

"JEWISH CEMETERY"

WEEK 24

"'If he is an honourable man he should either declare his intentions, or cease seeing you, and if you won't do this, I will. I will write to him, and I will tell Papa!' said Sonya resolutely."

LEO TOLSTOY

"And I saw no difference between God and our essential being, it seems to be all God, and yet my understanding took it that our essential being is in God, that is to say that God is God, and our essential being is a creation within God."

JULIAN OF NORWICH

It seems to be presumptuous to comment on Julian of Norwich's work as she was given such a deep understanding of God and existence. But, I suppose each of us is given our own understanding of existence. Reading and listening to others helps to enhance and define it. It helps to clarify some unanswered questions. It helps to throw light in the darkness, especially when we are going through a difficult patch. I am sure Julian went through some difficult patches in her life. In one section of her writings she describes a time when she oscillated between joy and deep sorrow, instantly changing from one to the other. So with us we go through sorrow to joy. We need to go down to go up. We need to feel our pain to be free of it. But freedom does come in the morning. In the morning of the spirit we emerge from our sorrow, fresh and new and lighter. At times of darkness we need people to pray for us, to keep the faith. When it is too painful to know that all is well, that is the time we need others to keep the faith for us. That is why it is good to be a member of any sort of a prayer community, and group of people who pray for each other is good. We all need to be held in prayer.

According to Julian of Norwich "Our essential being is a creation within God". Yes, I believe she is right.

"God wishes us to know that he safely protects us in both sorrow and joy equally. And to benefit his soul, a man is sometimes left to himself."

JULIAN OF NORWICH

Being "left to himself", feels awful. Joy goes out the window, peace seems far away on a distant planet, tension and distress take up residence in your mind and body. Ill ease prevails. God leaves us to flounder on our own. Sorrow washes over us like a tidal wave. But while we are still going through this, God is still with us. It is just that we do not feel it. During these times we need help from others. We need their love, their comfort, their faith and their prayers. It feels as if God has deserted us but he has not. We are protected from that which would break us, so long as we have placed ourselves in his care and under his protection, or someone else has. People who are truly broken have no one to pray for them. They have no one to ask God to take them into his care. So when we are well and able to, it is our spiritual duty to pray for others. Pray for all you know personally. Pray for everyone you meet or have contact with today and every day. Pray for all the people you read about in the papers or hear about on TV or radio. Pray for the dead you know and those who have no one to pray for them. Pray much. Pray often.

"Though we feel vengeful, quarrelsome and contentious, yet we are all mercifully enclosed in the kindness of God and in his gentleness."

JULIAN OF NORWICH

Everything that Julian of Norwich writes about in *Revelations of Divine Love* is so consoling. In a time when the prevailing ideas about God focused on his vengeance, sin and hell fire, God showed Julian that he loved us no matter what we did. It is up to us to let go of all vengefulness, quarrelsomeness and contentiousness, to surrender ourselves to God's care no matter what. God is still with us, no matter how badly we have behaved or how bad we feel. God has not left us. He is still with us, still surrounding us in his gentleness. It is up to us to stop fighting, fighting ourselves, fighting others, fighting the situation we find ourselves in, fighting life itself. Surrender, surrender, surrender. Surrender all to God, our lives, our wills, our friends, our relatives, our countries, our governments, the whole world. "All shall be well", Julian of Norwich says, and all is well. "All things work together for good for those who trust in the Lord."

"God forgives our sin when we repent, so he wants us to forget our sin of unreasonable depression and doubtful fear."

JULIAN OF NORWICH

Nowadays there is very little mention of sin. In times past there was, among Christians, a huge preoccupation, and for some, obsession, with sin. Because of that there has been a backlash against the use of the concept of sin and the word sin. It basically means wrong-doing. Sin for me today means not living in accordance with God's will for me, in either thought or action. Repentance is a process; first we need to admit to ourselves, to God and to another human being that we were wrong; second we need to be willing not to repeat it; third we need to make amends for any damage done. Once we have done that God has forgotten about it and so must we. God may remember it if we start to criticize others for something we do or have done ourselves.

Depression is really the lack of hope coupled with the turning of anger on ourselves. It is really bad for us. It is not in accordance with God's will for us. There is hope because God is with us and he wants only the best for us. Unreasonable depression is a sin against belief and self love. There is one form of depression which is reasonable and that is sadness or grief. This needs to be expressed, all losses needs to be mourned. Mourning is a healthy activity. Loss is a wound and every wound needs to weep.

Fear is the enemy. Fear is only functional when it is a short sharp warning. It is a command to 'Get out of here, you are not safe', to 'run for your life' or 'move quickly'. This kind of fear is essential, it warns us of danger and gives us the energy to take immediate action. Other than that, fear is a belief in the supremacy of a lower power or evil. Evil has not conquered the world, God has. On an individual basis, we need to conquer the evil within with God's help on a moment by moment, day by day basis.

"Man is naturally weak and foolish, and his will is smothered; and in this world he suffers storm and sorrow and woe, and the cause is his own blindness – he does not see God; for if he saw God continually he would have no evil feelings, nor any sort of impulse towards the craving which leads to sin".

JULIAN OF NORWICH

I like this quote, and all of Julian's book. It acknowledges that we are "weak and foolish". I am definitely aware of it at times. I have many times felt weak and vulnerable and beset by the world and the situations I find myself in. A lot of self-help books imply that we will have perfect happiness here on this earth if; we do x, y or z or if we change x, y or z. The truth is more basic. We are "naturally weak". It is part of our nature. No matter what we do, we come back to that, our own weakness and vulnerability. No matter how much money or resources are spent we cannot protect ourselves, our children, or our country completely from evil, our own or other peoples.

In Julian's revelations or insights, there is only one solution, which is to "see God continually". That is to see God in every happening, in everything. This is really challenging, to acknowledge God in all ways. How can you see God in everything? By staying close to God, by asking him to stay close to you, by trusting that when everything looks black that God is with you. We cannot see the big picture all the time. Pain seems to be a necessary part of life. All emotional pain needs to be felt. This is challenging as our natural inclination is to avoid it. We can only feel our deep emotional pain in God's gentle care and surrounded by love.

"For this is what was shown: that our life is all grounded and rooted in love, and without love we cannot live."

JULIAN OF NORWICH

Love casts out all fear. Fear and doubt are the enemy of love. God is the source of all love. Fear is the enemy forever raising its ugly head. Fear must be attacked at all costs, at every showing. Fear is not from God. Trust is from God. Trust God in all things. Trust God to protect you, your loves ones, your community, your country and the whole world. Stay close to God and you stay close to love. God does not hurt you. Life hurts and staying close to God heals. Healing often comes through tears. These are healing tears. God's healing love flows out of him and into us. Then the tears flow and flow and flow. Let it come, do not block it. All is well, all is well, all is well.

"VERITAS ET VITA"

WEEK 25

"As I watched the Orangemen's parade continue down the empty street, I felt like it was looking like it belonged in Disney World instead of on the streets of a city where the people has simply had enough and wanted to move on."

MICHAEL MOORE

"A glad giver pays little attention to the thing he is giving, but his whole desire and intention is to please and comfort the one to whom he gives it."

JULIAN OF NORWICH

"A glad giver." Do we always give with a glad heart? Do we give out of a sense of duty or obligation? Do we give in order to receive back, penny for penny, pound for pound. Give freely, give plenty, give to all who ask, give what is needed. Be a good giver, give of your time, give of your attention, give a smile, give a prayer. Every small gift is important. Sometimes it is the small gifts that are very precious. Once I was riding on an elephant. The elephant trainer moved off the path, picked a flower off a tree and gave it to me. The smallest gift can mean so much, a smile, a pat on the shoulder, a squeeze of a hand. The gift of a pen, a hairclip, a pin at the right time can be such a delight. Once I found a ten pound note on the ground, at a time when I and my children were close to having no food. It was such a welcome gift. It was a gift from God at the right moment. All gifts are from God. All babies conceived are a gift from God, to their natural parents, to their adoptive parents, to the world.

Be gracious receivers. Accept all gifts as a gift from God, even the smallest coin on the road, a single flower, a slice of bread, a cup of water. I once received a gift of a dress. At the time I had no need of it. Later on, an occasion came and the dress was perfect for it. This was during a period of my life when I would not have been able to buy a new dress. God provided for me, through a friend's kindness.

"He is the ground of our natural creation."
                              JULIAN OF NORWICH

What does this mean, our "natural creation"? I think this means ourselves, our bodies and the world we live in – the earth, air and all the plants and animals, water, rocks and soil. Does it mean God is the basis of our bodily self and our world as we perceive it? The ground is the basis, the foundation of something. So is God our foundation? If that is so why are we not living in perfect harmony within ourselves and between ourselves and our natural world? Would that not be what God wanted, desired, willed? Something went wrong.

In the Bible there is the story of the fall of Adam. He ate the fruit of the tree of knowledge. What knowledge? Why was knowledge bad for him? It could be that he saw evil for the first time and became afraid. He opened the door to fear, doubt and lack of trust and consciousness of lack of every sort. So our redemption is to close that door, let go of all evil, turn to God and trust absolutely.

"God always wants us to be secure in love, and peaceful and restful, as he is towards us."

JULIAN OF NORWICH

Is not this what we all want, "to be secure in love, and peaceful and restful"? Is not this what we are searching for even though we may not know it? When we are striving for a better job, a new house, a better sexual relationship, are we not really looking for peace, rest of soul and security within? We want these things and God wants to give them to us. So why do we not have them?

It says in the Bible "Ask and you shall receive". Perhaps we do not know what is best to ask for? Maybe we do not know what we really need or indeed what we would like? Perhaps the whole struggle in life is between wills; our will, God's will and the will of the evil one or our lower power? I believe that God wishes us to have our good, here and now. That is peace, perfect supply, perfect self-expression and perfect love. When our will and God's will is in perfect alignment, good things happen, heaven looks in. Good things happen for us and all we have contact with, and all God puts into our minds. Everything that happens is good even though it may not appear to be. Trust. In time you will see. Wonderful things are happening all the time. God is good. You are good. All is well.

"Of three properties of God, life, love and light... There is marvellous familiarity in life, gracious courtesy in love, and in light there is endless kindness."

JULIAN OF NORWICH

"Endless kindness"; this is what I need. How lovely it seems, "endless kindness". How I would like that "gracious courtesy" and "marvellous familiarity". This all sounds so wonderful. Is this available to us all? According to Dame Julian these are God's qualities. How can we get them? By staying close to God. Why am I in such pain so? I do not know. Pain is healing. All wounds need to be healed. We need to feel our own pain. You must go through the cross to the resurrection. The closer we get to God, the more our woundedness and brokenness comes to the forefront, to be healed. Our wounds can go back a long way even to our conception and back through the generations. They can go back seven generations. We are suffering for the unhealed wounds and unrepentant sins of our mother and father, our grandparents, our great grandparents, back to the seventh generation. If they did not receive healing, the wound carries over to the next generation. This carries on until someone turns themselves over to God totally and the healing begins, first of themselves then their family tree. The healing is painful, very painful, but joy comes in the morning. Do not give up. God is with you. All the help you need is at hand. "Keep right on till the end of the road."

"And in this personal request, it seemed that I stood in my own way, for I was not answered immediately."

JULIAN OF NORWICH

How often do we stand in our "own way"? How often are we our own worst enemy? Stubbornness, narrow mindedness, willfulness, obsessiveness, fearfulness and anxiety, all block us from seeing what is right for us. These processes block us from receiving God's peace and God's grace. Stand still, rest, listen to God's voice. It comes in the still quiet place of your heart. Wait, rest, listen. It comes as a whisper in the wind, as a gentle breeze on the night air. Stand still. God is around us. He is protecting us from evil and our own worst selves. Stand still, rest. Let God take care of you. You are precious in God's eyes, every hair on your head is counted. Let go of all your worries. Let him take care of all your concerns. Rest, rest, rest.

"The love of God never allows his chosen to lose their time, for all their trouble is turned into eternal joy."

JULIAN OF NORWICH

Trouble does come no matter what; no matter how hard you try to avoid it or work against it or change yourself. Trouble just comes. Sometimes it is the outside reflecting the inside. Other times it just is. It comes to challenge us, to help us grow, to teach us a lesson.

The "chosen" are those who surrender their lives to God, to their Creator, those who are willing to do God's will in their own lives. It does not matter whether they came to God through organized religion or not, once you are in God's care everything that happens to you, in every day of your life matters. It is important. It is for your ultimate good or someone else's. All suffering, all pain, all mistakes, all sin, can be used for or converted into good. All sin once admitted to and surrendered to God can be converted into compassion, first for ourselves and then for others. All mistakes are learning points. We need to feel our emotional pain in order to be released from its cause. Once we have felt our emotional pain we can then be cleansed of the effects of others' sin upon us. All unnecessary suffering can be let go of. All necessary suffering heals, cleanses and renews.

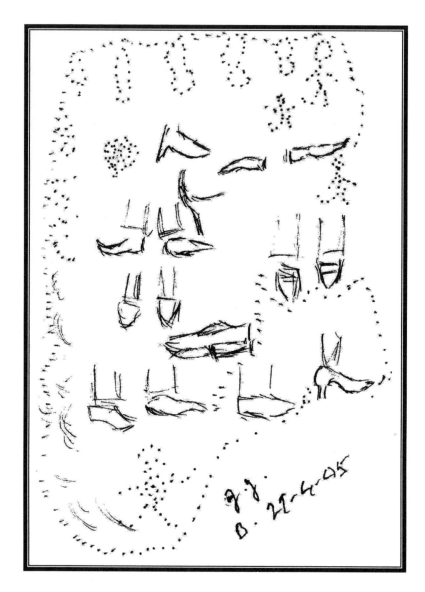

"FEET"

WEEK 26

"Hope is the thing with feathers-
That perches in the soul-
And sings the tune without the words-
And never stops - at all -"

EMILY DICKINSON

"For all things are good but sin, and nothing is wicked but sin. Sin is neither a deed nor a pleasure, but when a soul deliberately chooses to sin (which is punishment in God's eyes) in the end he has nothing at all."

JULIAN OF NORWICH

So what is sin? It is an unfashionable concept today. It is almost a taboo subject. In times past people focused on sin as a deed. This action was a sin or that action was a sin. Dame Julian says that sin is not a deed but a decision. It is something you choose. You choose not to turn to God. You choose to obey other commands. You choose to go along with the crowd. You choose to blindly follow an earthly authority. You choose self will instead of surrender to God's will.

The effects of sin are widespread: lack of basic necessities: pollution, overcrowding, disease, degradation, soul death (zombie-like people with no joy, no aliveness), mass fear, doubt, suspension, sudden death, violence between people, accidents and violent acts of nature.

God is good and all good comes from God. All destructiveness comes from the evil one and from our own lack of surrender to God.

"For our natural wish is to have God, and God's good wish is to have us."

JULIAN OF NORWICH

Deep down, we all need God. God loves us and wants us to come to him fully. God is the greatest of all lovers. For he knows us intimately, knows all our faults, all our mistakes and all our woundedness. He understands us completely and forgives us totally. We only need to turn to him for all the healing we need. We have free will. He will never force us. He has all his love and healing to give to us. We just have to turn to him and surrender our self will. Then everything that happens to us is for our ultimate good. Only good comes from contact with God no matter what. Praise God in all things and all situations for he makes all things new and good.

"Once again, the person like a man touched me; he gave me strength, 'do not be afraid,' he said, 'you are a man, specially chosen; peace be with you; play the man, be strong!'".

DANIEL 10:18-19

The "person like a man" was an angel, believed to be the archangel Gabriel. The angels are there for us to call on for guidance, for protection, for strength and healing. They connect up directly with God's power. God's power is so great that direct exposure to it is too much for us. We need to tap into small channels or filters or we would be blown away. The angels, the saints, the Eucharist all connect us straight to God, as do the hands of someone with the Holy Spirit flowing through them.

"You are a man." What does it mean to be a man? I do not know, not being a man myself. However it is important to be what you are, and not to try to be something you are not. What does it mean to be a woman to me? For a time in my life my womanhood expressed itself in the full reproductive cycle, of conception, pregnancy, birthing, breastfeeding and child-rearing. It was a positive experience for me overall. The most difficult part was the child-rearing. In rearing children you are confronted with the child within. In all of us our inner child is wounded or damaged in some ways.

So today what does womanhood mean to me? It means sensuality, giving and receiving; having fun, being safe and protected.

"Do not fear going forward slowly, fear only to stand still."
                                                CHINESE SAYING

This 'standing still' is staying put, not taking any risks, going round and round in circles, not making any decisions, staying on the same old treadmill. That is squashing any impulse to change, to explore, to strive for a better life. That is not daring to challenge anything or anyone. There is a certain security in not changing. The "devil you know is better than the devil you don't". However, if you do not change, other people and the world around us does. In nature there are no vacuums. There is constant change and constant use of space and things. Standing still in the context of this saying means going round in circles and coming back to the same place. This is repeated over and over again when there is too much fear of change or of taking a risk.

There is another standing still which is a waiting and a trusting. This is different. This is when you have done what you can and you leave the results to God. This is when you are not sure which way to go and you are awaiting for guidance and clarity.

Slow progress is good. Slow and steady. Sometimes it feels as if instead of going forward I am going round in circles. I am in fact returning to a similar place again but each time I deal with it better and quicker. So in actual fact instead of going round in circles I am going round in spirals and life is always interesting and challenging.

"If you have only one breath left, use it to say thank you."
                                             PAM BROWN

Nothing can be taken for granted. All that you are, all that you have, all that you see and sense has all been given to you and can all be taken away. Life itself, from the moment of conception to natural death, is a gift. It is the greatest gift of all from God. Do not take it for granted. As a gift, we do not have a right to it. No matter what the circumstances of our conception, our life is a gift.

God has also given us free will. We freely choose what to say, do and think. It is always our choice. Even if we believe we are being forced to say, do or not do something, we are still actually choosing to do it. When force is applied, we have a choice, conform or suffer the consequences. The choice is always ours.

Fresh air is a gift. Sunlight is a gift. Every piece of food we have to eat is a gift. Every thing any one has ever done for us is a gift. If you are feeling down today make a gratitude list. Afterwards you will feel better.

"Fear no evil because I have conquered evil. It has power to hurt only those who do not place themselves under my protection."

                                        TWO LISTENERS

The "I" referred to here is God. God will protect us from evil. But we must place ourselves under his protection. Someone else can ask for protection for us. I remember once getting a lift to a church from a man. Just as I was getting out of the car he asked me to pray for him. I said, "Pray for yourself". "I can't", he replied. Everybody needs to be prayed for. You can pray for your loved ones, people you have contact with, people you heard about, people who come into your mind. You do not need to have direct contact with a person in order to pray for them. This is wonderful. You do not even have to know their names. If we are alive today it is because someone somewhere at some time prayed for us and placed us under God's care. When people stop praying for each other disaster strikes, sudden death is common, disaster on a large scale is the result of prayerful neglect on a large scale. Disease, death, disaster; these are not God's will for us. Health, prosperity, wellness and love, these are God's will for us.

Fear is our enemy. Evil exists but we do not have to fear it. God has conquered fear and God is with us now. Stay close to God and fear vanishes. Keep turning to God. All is well. All is well.

"SWAN"

WEEK 27

"And God has given me to understand that there is but one thing that is of infinite value in His eyes, and that is love of God; love, love and once again, love; and nothing can compare with a single act of pure love of God." (Diary, #778)

SR M FAUSTINA KOWALSKA

"The very first step towards conquering temptation, is to see it as temptation."

TWO LISTENERS

What is temptation? Is an inducement, an inclination or an attraction to do wrong? Doing wrong is doing something which is harmful or destructive to yourself or others. Some things are obviously destructive, like killing another human being. Others are not so apparent and are often very individual. If you are addicted to a substance or a process there is often a trigger you need to avoid. The taste of sugar could trigger someone on an eating binge. The smell of alcohol could trigger someone else off on a drunken spree. We need to know ourselves and learn from our mistakes. Looking at pornographic material could set another off into sexual fantasy and inappropriate sexual behaviour. We need to fully and completely surrender ourselves, and every aspect of our being to God our Creator. We do not know ourselves completely but God does. We do not know our own motivations and all our weakness. God does, and still he loves us, in all our frailty. We need to surrender ourselves completely in order to protect ourselves and others from our worst selves.

All is well. All is well. God loves us, no matter how unloving we are or how unworthy of his love we are. His love is a precious gift, completely unearned by us but there for us at all times.

"Keep your spirit life calm and unruffled. Nothing else matters. Leave all to me.

TWO LISTENERS

This is very difficult. Life intervenes. Bills demand to be paid. The bus is late. The man I fancy ignores me. The cat eats your dinner. Death comes to visit. You get a flat tyre, a blood stain on your favorite dress, a scrape on your car or a brick through your window. Life is unpredictable and always throwing up challenges. How do you keep your "spirit life calm?" Acceptance. Bless everything that happens. It helps to keep close to God your Creator. But can you live in God's constant presence? Yes. Yes you can, and the more you are willing to do it, the more distractions and challenges come to you. It is the greatest love story of your life, the one from which all others flow. God is a jealous God, he likes to have our whole attention, love and gratitude. I do not know if he needs it, but he wants it. I believe the gift of our love freely given delights him greatly. He has given us free will, so that we would freely choose him. We can freely choose him, his presence, his will for us, his guidance and his power. When we choose freely we are acting in complete freedom, there is no coercion of any sort, no sense of duty or any fear operating. Fear and love cannot coexist, they cannot live side by side. They are complete opposites. God is love. Love yourself.

"You must pray. The way will open. God cares and His plans unfold. Just love and wait."

TWO LISTENERS

"Love and wait", this is difficult. The impulse is to do something. The thing to do is to place the matter in God's care and await guidance. This is a challenge. "You must pray." Praying brings you into God's presence. Pray more. Prayer itself brings peace. You cannot continually talk to God without peace coming eventually. All disease, all ill ease comes because of distance from God. All is well. Prayer helps the person praying and the person prayed for. It is a circle of love. Love surrounds you, it goes between you and God. It then spreads to the people prayed for. The circle widens and widens as you are led to pray for more and more people; for both, the living and the dead, those you have contact with and those you do not. Good always comes from prayer. Prayer is the opening of the door to God's power, the power to heal, to love and to guide. Prayer opens the door and directs the beam of healing power to where it needs to go. Tap into this vast well of power and love. It is there for us all to use. It is there for the asking. Use it. Use it. Pray often. Pray continually. Pray. Pray. Pray.

"Face each day with love and laughter. Face the storm."
                                        TWO LISTENERS

Face everything. Face yourself. Face your past. Face your family tree. Face your history. Face your culture. Face all your relationships. Face all your finances. Face all your faults. Face all your assets and good qualities. Face life. Face death, your own and others. Face the day. Face the night. Face your health. Face your sexuality. Face your fertility. Face your talents. Face your failures. Face your successes. Face God. Face down the devil. Face the weather. Face the leaky tap. Face all there is to face today. Do what you have to do today. Today is the only day you have to live well. Face your hair. Face your teeth. Face the boil on your bum, if you can! Face whatever you need to face today then laugh.

Life is full of obscurity, oddness and ridiculousness. Laugh at yourself. Laugh at life. Laughter releases tension and keeps you young and healthy. God is good and he has a great sense of humour.

"Man often suffers loss through lack of appreciation."
FLORENCE SCOVEL SHINN

We lose the thing we do not care about or value. To appreciate things or people means to value them, to be grateful for them, to see the good in them, to be happy to have them.

What do I appreciate? Myself, my life, my body, my health, my children , their lives, their health, my friends, all the kindness I have received in my life, all the good times, all the unusual, exciting and wonderful experiences of my life so far. I appreciate fun and laughter, sunshine and light, the earth and all that grows on it and lives on it. I appreciate the sky and the sea and all the natural flow of water. I appreciate colour and healthy smells and the feel of warm air on my skin. I appreciate fresh air, a comfortable chair and being able to stretch out my legs. I appreciate cotton and silk and woolen fabrics. I appreciate good service and the kindness of strangers. I appreciate being able to see the sun rise and the sun set. I appreciate blue skies and warm blue seas. I appreciate flowers of every kind. I appreciate beautiful cars and powerful motor bikes. I appreciate the sight of small babies and the sight of lovers of all ages.

"No man can attract money if he despises it."
　　　　　　　　FLORENCE SCOVEL SHINN

Money is important. Everybody in modern life needs it, either to use directly or to be used on their behalf. Money is energy. Money and energy go hand in hand. Many people think you need money first before making a decision and taking action. No, make your decision first. Then start preparing for the action. Then money comes and attaches itself to the enterprise, if it is from God. You must love the thing you want to attract. If you want to attract money you must like it, respect it, spend it freely. Do not be afraid to let money go out. Spend with wisdom. Enjoy paying your bills. Enjoy receiving money. Accept every gift no matter how small, even one penny.

If you want to attract, a man or a woman, look on all men or woman kindly. See the good in them, value their masculinity or femininity. Amazing things will start to happen. Sexual attraction has nothing to do with age, size or appearance. Men and women attract what they appreciate, what they expect and what they fear. If you expect rejection you will get it. If you expect sexual attraction, love and kindness you will get it. So expect the best and you will get it. Accept nothing less. At the perfect time it will come. Love all and it will return to you. Love is the mightiest force, it dissolves everything in its path.

"BIRDS OF A FEATHER"

WEEK 28

"I thought I would die of joy and happiness. I felt the separation of my spirit from my body. I felt totally immersed in God. I felt I was snatched up by the Almighty, like a particle of dust, into unknown expanses." (Diary, #439)

SR M FAUSTINA KAWALSKA

"Simplicity is the keynote of my kingdom. Choose simple things always."

TWO LISTENERS

Simplicity is not easy in this complicated world we live in today. All the processes of life are getting more and more complicated and difficult. It is very easy nowadays to fall into debt. It is easier and easier to break laws unknowingly and get fined or worse. There is less and less privacy and, more and more intrusiveness, by officialdom, into your private life. How do you keep life simple? Choosing the easy option is not always the best. What is initially easy can become very complicated. In modern life it seems to be important to stand back and research everything before committing to anything. Advertising and sales techniques are very slick and things are rarely what they seem. Great discernment is needed. Pray for this. The loyalty of the person you are dealing with is to the company or employer they work for, not with the client or customer. Pray for the right person to answer the phone, or reply to your e- mail, visit or letter. Prayer can move mountains.

"I am your Shield. No buffers of the world can harm you. Feel that between you and all scorn and indignity, is a strong shield. Practice feeling this until nothing has the power to spoil the inward peace."

TWO LISTENERS

This is so necessary. There is a great deal of hatred, malice and anger in the world. Misery likes company. People in pain and darkness hate to see others in the light. These people, spew out venom and malice over those they are jealous of. If you are walking in the light on a spiritual path you are bound to be attacked again and again. It is not personal. The powers of darkness hate to see the power of light in action, and attack. It feels personal because it is you that is being personally attacked. First ask for, and then feel the strong shield of protection around you. Know that you are safe, and that all is well. God has the victory and God is with you. You are on the winning side.

"Spend more time in soil-preparing. Prayer fertilizes soil. There is much to do in preparation."

TWO LISTENERS

Prayer fertilizes the soul. Prayer is talking to God. Meditation is listening to God. Staying close to nature helps us to understand God. Nature is God's creation, it is through his power and spirit that it came into being. In nature there is a time for everything and everything comes at its appointed time. So also with us, there is a right time for everything. There is a time for falling in love and a time for having children. There is time for growing up and time for yourself. There is a time for learning and a time to apply your knowledge and skills. There is a time for going and a time for coming. There is a time for standing firm and a time for letting go. There is a time for standing still and a time for action. There is a time for prosperity and a time for lack. There is a time to be born and a time to die. Trust, all will come at the appointed time, all the dearest wishes of your heart will be fulfilled.

"Attachments can only thrive in the darkness of illusion."
ANTHONY DE MELLO

Clinging, wanting: wanting people, things and situations to be the way you want them to be; holding on for dear life to a relationship, an idea, a house, a car or a belief; trying to force solutions; to make things the way you want them to be; therein lies disaster, disillusionment and constant unhappiness. If you are miserable today you are attached to some person, thing or idea. What is causing you to be unhappy today? What idea are you holding unto? Once you can identify it let it go. Just let it go. Do you want your husband or wife to be more loving, more understanding? Let go of the idea, let go of the desire. Accept them as they are for today. Love will come to you from some other source. It may even be a cat or a dog that will love you today, or a smile from a passing child or a gentle warm breeze on your face. Just let go of wanting it from one person, one source. All you need for today is there for you. Tomorrow is another day. Let tomorrow take care of itself.

"Love that first springs in the heart through your contact with the Real."

ANTHONY DE MELLO

What is "the Real"? Is it the real you? Is it your real self? Is it the reality of your life today? Is it what is really going on around you in society or in nature? Or is it the source of all goodness and light? How do we contact this realness, this reality? It is a challenge. I think we need to stand back from ourselves and see what we are doing. Why am I reacting like I am? What am I reacting to? What do I really feel now? In order to stand back and observe ourselves and others we need quiet. We need to quiet the Chatterbox in our heads. Find a method of meditation that works for you. Put yourself in God's care first. For some, sitting in the presence of the Blessed Sacrament in a Catholic church is good, when it is available. Rhythmical activities like, walking, cycling or rowing out in the fresh air are good. They are moving meditations. Any kind of rhythmical activity, is good to calm the mind, like juggling or hitting a ball against a wall repeatedly. Formal meditation or prayer groups are good. They get rid of the rubbish in our heads and calm us down. Then we can start to look at what is really there. Bon voyage.

"When you are too long separated from Nature, your spirit withers and dies because it has been wrenched from its roots."

ANTHONY DE MELLO

This is so true. Nature is a reflection of God's mind. We are made from the same Creator. Fresh air is the best air for us to breath. Natural scenes are the best for us to contemplate. Looking in the long distance in natural surrounding is the most restful for our eyes. Breastfeeding is the easiest way to bond with and nurture your baby. The society we live in today and the nature of our lives makes it difficult to establish and maintain breastfeeding. Once established, it is good for a woman's body and the total wellbeing of the baby. Contact with nature heals us and teaches us. It teaches us about God and it teaches us about our own human nature. Nature is bountiful and so is God. In nature there is a time for everything: there is a time for planting and a time for harvesting; there is a mating season and a season for birthing; there is a time for resting and a time for action; there is a time for living and a time for dying. Left to its own devices, nature is always in balance. Each species has all it needs for survival. Man alone can dominate the earth. All other species are in balance with each other. Our most vulnerable point is our ego, our desire to control the earth and our own environment. With out God's grace we would probably have destroyed ourselves and our planet long ago. God is with us. God is with us, all the time.

"RESTAURANT"

WEEK 29

"And who or what shall fill his place?
Whither will wanderers turn distracted eyes
For some fixed star to stimulate their pace
Towards the goal of their enterprise?"

THOMAS HARDY

"If your spirit becomes unclogged and your senses open you will begin to perceive things as they really are and to interact with reality and you will be entranced by the harmonies of the universe."

ANTHONY DE MELLO

This sounds wonderful. So what clogs up your spirit? Obsessions, addictions, wanting things and people to be the way you want them to be, set dysfunctional beliefs and attitudes of mind; letting 'should' rule your life: "she should be like this", or "he should do that", or "I should not be this way". People and things are the way they are, just for today. People and things are the way they are now at this moment and perhaps for today and many more days to come. A great freedom comes from accepting, people and things just as they are for now. This is the way things are for now. Nothing lasts for ever, it will pass. Now I may be tired, now I may be in danger, now I may have somewhere to stay, now I have food available to me, now I may be in pain. It is just for now, just for this moment, maybe for today maybe not. God is with us always, every moment of every day of our lives. Lean on him.

"Understand your unhappiness and it will disappear. What results is a state of happiness."

ANTHONY DE MELLO

So what truly makes you unhappy? For adults it is not other people. Other people have no power over the state of your mind, heart and spirit, unless you give it to them. Why are you unhappy now at this moment? It is not other people. You may think it is but it is not. If you say, "it's him, he is so cruel", or "it's her, she's so mean", these people are not the cause of your unhappiness. It is not what they did or did not do that caused you unhappiness but how you reacted to it.

So what are you saying to yourself when you react to other people's behaviour? "I am no good", "I deserved that", "nobody loves me", "nobody will ever love me", "I am all alone", "I cannot protect myself", "nothing good ever happens to me", "I am stupid", "I can't do anything right". Dig deep, look at what you are really saying to yourself. Whatever it is, it is not true. Replace the negative statement with a positive one. Repeat the positive statement over and over again, to yourself, on paper and out loud. You are a wonderful unique person. You are special. You are perfect just as you are. You were conceived as a perfect idea in God's mind. Let go of all that hampers you and weighs you down. You will feel lighter and look younger.

"Every time you strive to improve on nature by going against it, you will damage yourself, because nature is your very being."
ANTHONY DE MELLO

This is so true. All the artificial interference in our reproductive cycle is all coming back to bite us now. Long term use of chemical contraception in some women is leading to the early onset of menopause and infertility. These chemicals tell the body 'don't ovulate'. After years of this it gets the message and shuts down the woman's ovaries permanently. The modern answer to that is more artificial manipulation of our reproductive system. This has lead to conception outside the human body, genetic engineering and cloning. This will come back to bite us unless we stop all this interference in a perfectly balanced and working, natural reproductive system. If you assist nature and go along with it, it will reward you with great bounty. Population control had led to fewer and fewer children being born and more and more people in the older age groups. A high proportion of older people puts a big strain on the resources of a country. We interfered with the balance of nature and now we are paying for it.

God is with us and to the extent that we let him, he will turn our lives, our communities and our countries around.

"Effort may change the behavior but it does not change the person."

ANTHONY DE MELLO

Effort comes from self-will. Our will be done. It is important when we have a job to complete. It helps us to pick ourselves up and continue to the end. It helps us to do the practical things of life, the routine things of life like brushing our teeth, getting dressed, housework, shopping, food preparation. You cannot change yourself or another adult by force of will. You can control your own behaviour for a time with a lot of effort. But real lasting change comes from within. It comes about by the grace of God, the power of God working in us and upon us. God can only work on or in us when we surrender our self-ill to him, her, it. When we surrender our total selves to him then he can start to work on us. Truth dawns on us. Awareness comes slowly. Old beliefs get smashed to pieces. New ones replace them for a time. God is greater than all our conceptualizations of him. Our puny mind cannot encompass all God's creation. We are but a speck of dust in the universe. But very important to God, because he came to dwell within us. He wants us to freely choose him and only him. He loves us and he wants us to freely love him, wholeheartedly and unreservedly.

"It is enough for you to be watchful and awake."
ANTHONY DE MELLO

What do you need to be watchful of? You need to be watchful of everything around you, everything in the present, all your own reactions to people and situations, all your own emotions. Feel your emotions, let them come and stand back from them. Where are they coming from? Are they coming from the past or from the present situation? Step back and have a look at them. Life is not about other people, their behaviour, their reactions, it's about you, your relationship with your maker and the world as it is.

What does it mean to be awake? It means to be present in the present. It means to be aware of what is going on around you, in your immediate surroundings, in your neighbourhood, in your country, in the natural world, in the people that you deal with and in yourself.

Where are you now? Look around you. What do you see? What do you hear? How does your body feel? All is well. You have survived to this day, to this moment. Praise God.

"Those who are truly free cannot sin as God cannot sin."
ANTHONY DE MELLO

What does this mean? What does it mean to be "truly free"? Free of what? Could it be freedom from all negative feelings of, resentment, grief, sadness, despair, fear, repressed anger or despondency? Could it be freedom from all negative thinking and repressed emotions? Those who are truly free are free to live in the present, to see what is in front of them, to feel their feelings as they arise and to see people clearly with full understanding and compassion.

What does it mean to sin? Does it mean to hurt or destroy yourself or others? If your feelings are fully alert and your senses are alive, you will feel the spirit that unites all created matter. All created matter was created by God and God's spirit is within all. In the Bible there is mention of stones crying out. If stones can cry then surely the spirit of God must be strong in all plants and animals and of course humans. So how, if you are in contact with the spirit of God within you, could you deliberately kill or damage any other living thing, unless it is for food when necessary.

If you are fully alive as a human being then you can connect with the humanity of all human beings and could not deliberately hurt or damage them, unless it was absolutely necessary for survival.

"THE EYE"

WEEK 30

"And alien tears will fill for him
Pity's long-broken urn,
For his mourners will be outcast men,
And outcasts always mourn."

OSCAR WILDE

233

"Real oppression comes... from your computer whose programming destroys your peace of mind the moment outside circumstances fail to conform to its demands."

ANTHONY DE MELLO

It is not what happens to us that counts, but how we react to it. What is our programming? Our programming is our core beliefs. It is what we believe the world should be, how we expect things to be. They are our beliefs about ourselves and the world. We absorbed these beliefs as children from what was said repeatedly such as "you are stupid", "you always get things wrong", "it's not safe outside", "the dark is dangerous". Our deeply held beliefs are stored in the subconscious. They are put there in childhood. They seep into us from our parents, our care givers, past generations, present cultures and from our own culture and personal experience. What are our own deeply held beliefs? How do we access them? Observation; observe yourself, stand back and look at what you are doing and how you are reacting to other people. The answers are all within. You have a right and a duty to understand yourself and you alone. Other people's motives are not your business. Know yourself and you will know the world.

"Man is weak by his own hand, for he has refashioned God's law into his own confining manner of life."

KAHLIL GIBRAN

Our lives are fashioned by our minds. It is in our minds that all unhappiness lies. When you look at strangers who pass you in the street, what tells you if they are happy or not? It's their faces. Unhappiness can be seen in their faces. Preoccupation, distraction, repressed anger, fear, bitterness, resentment, being totally out of it, all show in a person's face. Take these away and you have lightness, alertness, joy, awareness and responsiveness. All unhappiness is in your mind.

Your mind has many layers. It is the stuff that is operating below the surface that can cause so much trouble. Below the surface are unexpressed emotions, deeply held personal beliefs, attachments to ideas, dreams or ideals and painful memories. Painful memories are stored in the body as well as the deeper recesses of our mind. These memories can be accessed through the body.

We need to stop running, live in the present, be where we are now, allow our feelings to surface, let go of our attachments, step back and see what our beliefs are, and let go of the false ones.

Be happy now. Now is the moment.

"An escape from misunderstanding, from yourself... whither can you flee! To the Eternal God your refuge. Till in his immensity you forget your smallness, meanness, limitations."

TWO LISTENERS

Fleeing from yourself. Are not we all fleeing from ourselves? What are addictions to food, to relationships, to drugs, to alcohol, to gambling or to working, but a fleeing from yourself? All obsessions and addictions block feelings, and prevent us being present to ourselves. When we are totally present to ourselves then our suppressed pain surfaces. It is easer to suffer the pain of addiction than to be truly with ourselves and feel all our unfelt feelings: the feeling of shame and guilt, the feeling of deep sorrow and grief for all our losses, the feeling of hurt and betrayal, the feeling of anger and fear, the feeling of violation and desecration or the truly terrible feeling of abandonment that only the child in us can feel in its totality.

It is safe to be whatever you are, to feel your feeling, in God's arms. Allow whatever is there to surface. All is well. All is well. You are all right. You are safe. All is well. All is well.

"You can only be free when even the desire of seeking freedom becomes a harness to you, and when you cease to speak of freedom as a goal and a fulfillment."

KAHLIL GIBRAN

Desire is an attachment. An attachment is wanting: wanting a specific person, thing or situation. It is you deciding that such and such a person will make you happy or such and such a person behaving in a certain way will make you happy or such and such a job, home, event or object will make you happy. Other people, things and situations do not in themselves make you happy. Happiness is an inside job. A person who is not always wanting, can enjoy what they have. They can enjoy what is available to them today. They can enjoy all the wonderful things in the world around them: the beauty of nature, the kindness of strangers, the wonder of modern inventions, the delight of young children, the presence of lovers young and old, the eccentricity of some people's dress and behaviours, the light of the sun and the feel of warm air caressing your skin. Let go of all your worries and concerns now. Let them all go. Enjoy what is beautiful today.

"Holiness is not an achievement, it is a Grace. A Grace called Awareness, a grace called Looking, Observing, Understanding."
ANTHONY DE MELLO

The awareness, looking, observing and understanding referred to here is of yourself first. It is being aware of how you behave and react to other people and situations. For myself I would like to change the word, "holiness", to the word "wholeness". It is your whole self working in harmony with God, nature and your true self. Being the self you were meant to be. Being the self God conceived you to be without any woundedness, distractions, disease or malfunction of any kind. I do believe we were meant to be whole, healthy, functioning, adapting human beings, capable of living life to the full and being joyous, happy and free. We have been affected by the sins of our parents who were in turn affected by the sins of their parents and so on right back the line. We have also been affected by the culture we grew up in and the circumstances of our childhood. We reach adulthood as wounded people. We need healing. For this we need to surrender ourselves to God our Creator and he will arrange our healing for us. The people, places and things that are for our benefit will come into our lives, in sequence, in perfect order and we will be well. As well as we are willing to be. All that you need is within. You are fundamentally perfect today. Just accept it. Be your perfect self today. God loves you, love yourself.

"So spend some time seeing each of the things you cling to for what it really is, a nightmare."

ANTHONY DE MELLO

This covers the people, things and situations, ideas and dreams we cling to. What do you cling to? Is it a relationship or the idea of a relationship, or a desire to have a relationship go a certain predetermined way? Is it a job, a house, or the idea of a perfect house, job, public transport system, fairness for all, fairness for yourself? Look at what you are clinging to most virulently at the moment. How much pain is that idea, that desire causing you? Just let go of it. Every time it comes into your mind let it go. Let it go with love. Hand your desire over to God your Creator. There may be nothing wrong with your desire but wanting it is causing you pain. It is closing your mind to other options. It is closing your mind to the beauty of today, to all the good that is in your life today. If you desire a baby of your own, there may be lots of children in your life who need your attention. If you desire one man, you may not notice others who desire you. All is well. God is with us. Go with God.

"POTS OF MONEY"

WEEK 31

"Let me not pray to be sheltered from dangers but to be fearless in facing them."

RABINDRANATH TAGORE

Today I have no quote. It is a hard day for me. My head aches. My body is full of tension. I need to let go of all tension, all unanswered questions, all desire to have the things I am involved with work out. They will work out one way or the other and I will make good decisions when I have to. I need to let go of trying to work things out in advance. Today I need to live in the day. Stand still and let God work things out. I am willing to do my part. There is nothing more to do. The sun is shining. There is soft music playing in the background. I have a comfortable seat to sit in. I have a place to stay in tonight and money in the bank. My children are well. I am alive. I feel my dog Harry near me today. He always comes when I am down or troubled. Harry has been dead for a few years now but his spirit comes to me whenever I need him.

"You shall be free indeed
when your days are
not without a care nor
your nights without a want and a grief,
But rather when these things girdle your life and
yet you rise above them
naked and unbound."

KAHLIL GIBRAN

Today I am in a place of stress and tension. So where is it coming from? It is inside of me. What is triggering it? Fear. Fear of what? Is it disapproval, verbal abuse, physical violence, homelessness, dependency, violation of personal freedom and space? I feel under threat.

All is well. I will make the right decisions. I am in God's care. All is well. All is well.

"Where does the enemy attack? The fortress, the stronghold, not the desert waste."

TWO LISTENERS

The enemy of spiritual growth and healing has many names, Satan, The Devil, The Enemy, Evil, The Evil One, The Powers of Darkness, The Forces of Destruction and many more names. In this world there are two powers at work, the power of creation, growth, health and well-being, and the power of deception, destruction, distraction, and disease. At any one point in time you cannot serve two masters, you can only serve one or the other. With whom do you align yourself with today, the power of light or the power of darkness? Today and everyday for the rest of my life, I align myself fully with God, the Creator of heaven and earth and all living things.

"And you will understand how true it is that every one who stops clinging to brothers, sisters, father, mother or children, land or houses... is repaid a hundred times and gains eternal life."

ANTHONY DE MELLO

The key word here is "clinging". When you cling to someone you want it, you want them or it to be a certain way. Give up clinging. Give up wanting. All that you need, all that you would wish for, will come your way in God's own time. Bless everybody that crosses your path. Bless every situation that you are involved in. Bless every thing that happens to you, no matter how negative or destructive it appears to be. It happened for a purpose, a good purpose for you to learn or grow from it or perhaps for the others involved in it to learn and grow from it too. You do not need to understand all. You do not need to understand other people's reasons or motives. It is not always given to you to understand other people's or outside situations, but you will always be given an understanding of yourself and your motivation if you desire it and ask for it.

"Happy events make life delightful but they do not lead to self-discovery and growth and freedom. That privilege is reserved to the things and persons and situations that cause us pain."

ANTHONY DE MELLO

Are you in pain now? Rejoice. Pain in your body is a signal that something is wrong, but pain in your heart is a sign of growth. Something is coming to the surface, some loss, some grief, some buried anger, some deep wound. That is good. Pain is caused by the breaking through of buried emotions like a seed pushing up its shoots into the air. After it breaks through it bears fruit in due season.

Allow the pain to surface. Let it come. Feel your feelings. Stay with it, you are completely safe. God is with you, holding you gently in his arms. All is well. All is well. All is well.

"There is only one cause of unhappiness: the false beliefs you have in your head, beliefs so widespread, so commonly held, that it never occurs to you to question them."

ANTHONY DE MELLO

Unhappiness starts in your head, makes its way down to your heart and into your body. What do you really believe? Life is unfair! Everybody else gets a good deal and I get a raw deal! I will never have enough. They are out to get me. I will always be done – cheated or conned. All men are bad. All women are bad. What do you really believe about life, about living?

So how can you change your destructive beliefs? First of all you must identify them. That is really the difficult bit. You need to stand back from yourself and your life to see it clearly. You can stand back from your life by going on retreats, by going on pilgrimages to holy places, by going up a mountain on your own, by taking a long walk by a beach, by attending any form of group therapy sessions. Talking time out from your ordinary life and relationships is good, in fact it is essential to maintain total well-being. While taking time out from yourself you need to listen, listen to yourself, listen to others, listen to the still, small voice of God. Write down your thoughts and your beliefs will shine through. Once these are identified all negative ones can be changed to positive ones by replacing the negative ones with a positive affirmation. For example a belief in lack can be replaced by the statement: "There is an abundant supply for my every need". Choose you own affirmations, the ones that seem right to you.

"WATCHING ME WATCHING YOU"

WEEK 32

"You witness other people's grief and anger and excitement and joy, and you also feel it; however rather than becoming part of the scene, you take away with you a sense of wonder that survival and humanity are stronger than violence and suffering."

KATE ADIE

"All there is, is a keen, alert, penetration, vigilant awareness that causes the dissolution of all one's foolishness and selfishness, all one's attachments and fears."

ANTHONY DE MELLO

There is a state of well-being when you have let go of all your attachments and face all your fears. However, I wonder if we ever really reach this state completely or continuously for very long! Once we are in God's care we are continuously being challenged. In time the periods of well-being and clarity increase and lengthen.

The people and situations that frighten us are repeatedly being presented to us to deal with. Each time with God's help, we deal with it better, quicker. Attachments that cause us pain are being brought to our attention, we are being asked to let go. Letting go is painful. The pain of letting go is so intense it can feel, for a time, stronger than the pain of attachment. But if you stick with it, it will ease and finally go. The result is a sense of newfound freedom and lightness. Letting go of an attachment to a person, place, thing or idea is challenging. It can feel like a death. Doubts and fears can attack. "Am I doing the right thing?" "Maybe I should go back?" "Why am I in this situation?" "What have I done to deserve this?" Letting go is painful but good and any kind of support you can muster at this time helpful. The pain will pass, there is light at the end of the tunnel. God is with you holding you gently in his arms. All is well. All is well.

"Plenty, plenty, plenty."

JOANNA JORDAN

There is plenty in this world for everyone. Abundance is nature's way and God's way. All we have to do is believe it and turn away from thoughts of lack. Lack is not from God. Every time a poverty thought comes into your head, knock it on the head! There is plenty there for all. You do not need to know where it will come from or how it will come but it will come if you believe and keep alert for it. Think thoughts of plenty. Think perfection. Ask for perfection for yourself and others. Perfection is God's way. God is not cheap, mean or inadequate in any way. He wants the best for you: the best occupation, the best accommodation, the best relationships, the best health, the best lifestyle, the best clothes, the best children, the best method of transportation, the most loving of people in your life, the best teachers, nothing but the best.

Once you are in God's care, everybody that crosses your path has a gift for you, some help, guidance or a lesson to be learned. If you find a person difficult, the difficulty is within yourself and they are there to teach you. Bless them. Learn your lessons quickly or the lesson will be repeated until you do. Pray for all. Pray for all you meet or have contact with in any way. They need your prayers and you need to pray for them. They are there for a purpose. No one crosses your path accidentally. All is well. All is well.

"At that moment, I knew I was not going to let fear get the best of me. I would find a way to rid myself of the negativism that prevailed in my life."

SUSAN JEFFERS

Fear is not from God. The only healthy fear is a warning. A sudden painful feeling that says, "Oh, do not go there", or a strong alarm bell that says "get out of here now!", or, "run now", or, "move it quickly". It is sudden and sharp and persistent if ignored. This is God letting you know quite clearly "this is not safe for you".

What do I fear today? I fear going home to an empty house. Face the fear. Feel the fear and do it anyway. Go home face the empty house. Embrace the emptiness. What else do I fear? I am afraid of making mistakes. I am afraid to waste a lot of energy doing the wrong thing. So what if it is wrong. How do you know anyway? If things do not turn out as you expect, that does not mean you failed in your endeavor. No one knows the good your actions may have done. No one knows the effects of all the things they do. If you are in God's care, he will use you for good in spite of your own intentions. Amazing things could be happening without you knowing it. Trust God. All is well. All is well. You are divinely protected at all times. You are surrounded by angels at all times. Every step you take is divinely ordained. All is well. All is very well indeed.

"If I am not making mistakes, I can be sure I am not learning and growing."

SUSAN JEFFERS

Mistakes are part of living. They just say "not this way", "not that" or "not now". They make us stop and rest, stop and think again. They are just little corrections along the way of life. They say "there is something to learn here".

The only way to avoid mistakes is to do nothing and that in itself is a mistake. Sometimes we keep making the same mistake over and over again. Then it is time for a long sit down. It is a pattern, a pattern of some dysfunction. It is time to ask yourself "what is going on here?" Keep the focus on yourself. It is you that is repeating the pattern no one else. What ever is causing this in yourself needs to be changed. Very often just seeing what is going on is enough to change the pattern. Mistakes are part of living. If you are not making mistakes and readjustments you are not living.

At the end of the day we must work out our own salvation with God's help. Life is a puzzle and it is up to us to solve our own particular piece of it. Life is a challenge, an unending challenge. Suicide is very sad, because among other things the suicide victim has given up the challenge, has thrown in the towel or may be they have gone as far as they can on their own steam. They have exhausted all their own resources and have not tapped into the vast reservoir of God's power.

"Disappointment may make you miss the good that can come out of every situation in which you put yourself."

SUSAN JEFFERS

You make a decision to do something and it does not turn out to be as you expected it. The picture you had in your mind does not match up with the reality. Throw away the picture. Accept where you are for now. Look for all the good in your present situation. Maybe you need to change, maybe not. Write down all the good in your present situation. Literally count your blessings, write them all down. Accept the consequences of your decision. If you made a decision and took the action for change then accept the consequences of it. That brought you to where you are now. Once you are in God's hands all change is for the best. It would not have happened unless good could come of it for yourself or others. Every change brings with it an energy, a positive energy, good in motion. Stagnation is the worst thing. Stagnant water breads disease and stinks after a while. You do not need to be changing addresses, jobs or relationships all the time but change something. Clear out all the rubbish in your home, in your thinking, in your garden, in your life. Go forward fearlessly into the future. Go now. Take action today.

"Action is the key to your success. You have to do something to make your real life match your visualizations."

SUSAN JEFFERS

There is a time to act and a time to stand still. The closer you get God, your Creator, the more you will know when it is time to act or time to stand still. Some times you can get stuck in inaction. Sometimes we know we need to leave this job, this marriage, this place but we do not have the courage to take the action, for today. The only way to get unstuck is to start with the simplest, easiest, smallest action. Make an enquiry, start looking into your options. Write a to do list. List all the things you need to do in order to accomplish your plan. Start with the first thing on the list. Maybe even buying a pen and notebook is the place to start. Do something. Make a start no matter how small. Break it down into small manageable actions and start. Start today. Do not delay. The Chinese have an old saying: "A journey of a thousand miles begins with the first step". Just take one action now. God is with you.

"BROWNS"

WEEK 33

"Don't over think. If it looks like a duck and it quacks like a duck – it's a duck."

BEN MEZRICH

"When you stay centered there is nothing to fear. You are tapping your source of power, and everything is okay."

SUSAN JEFFERS

The centre of your being is a place of safety. In your centre all is well. Every time you are thrown off centre, knocked sideways or put down you have left your safe place. The still centre of your being is where God resides. He resides in all of us. That is why murder is a terrible crime. A human being murdered is God destroyed. No matter how evil a person's behaviour is, there is still a small centre within them, where God resides. The breath of life comes from God.

Every moment you live in contact with your centre is a good moment, a moment of joy and peace, a moment of right thinking and right action. The whole struggle of life is in being distracted from your centre and going back again, over and over again. Some people live most of their lives off centre. All evil is a distraction. Keep your focus on yourself and God, your Creator. All is well. All is well. God is with us. God is with us all the time.

"Remembering that God is my source, we are in the spiritual position of having an unlimited bank account."

                                        JULIA CAMERON

Do not limit God. God is infinite. There are no limits. All love, all the riches of the world, all the healing you need or even want is there for you. Do not limit God's power. It is vast and eternal. Accept the way things are for today. Enjoy all the good things in your life today. Apprecate everything you have. Take nothing for granted. Know that there is more to come: more money, more love, more beauty, more wonder, more health, more wisdom, more fun, more laughter, more joy, more excitement, more changes and more life. Take everything as a gift, a gift from God. Hold onto nothing except your friendship with God. Rejoice and be glad, delight in all good things. Enjoy the wonder of life. See God working in your life and in all ways. Look at the sky and know that God is with us. Let go of all doubt and fear. Go forward fearlessly into the future. Go forward. All is well. All is well.

"All too often, it is audacity and not talent that moves an artist to center stage."

JULIA CAMERON

Audacity is a wonderful quality. To be audacious is to be bold, fearless, brave without hesitation. Just do it. Just do it. Jump in, feet first and touch the bottom. No fear, just jump in and do it. Sink or swim. Life is for living. Be bold. Go forward fearlessly. Take the risk. God is with you. Reach for your dream. Put a foundation under your castles in the air. Boldness has magic in it. You may get bumped a bit or scraped but in the end you will be all the better for it.

Believe in yourself. Go for it. God is with you. There are angels at your feet. A safety net will appear to protect you. Just do it; victory to the brave, victory to the brave.

"Serious art is born from serious play."

JULIA CAMERON

How could this be? What is play? Play is fun, play is fantasy, play is relaxed, play is safe, play can be intensely serious, intensely involved. In play you use your imagination, your controller goes out the window, you can make your own rules and break them. Play is never boring. Once children become bored with play they stop. Play is always intensely fascinating and satisfying. In play we make believe, we allow our fantasy full reign. Play is good. Play is immediate. When we play we are totally in the moment, totally alive, we are in a world of wonder.

Have a play date today, with yourself, with your child within. Fly a kite, dress up for a dream date, buy a hula hoop and use it, do a summersault on the grass, blow bubbles, put on some music and dance. Have fun. Enjoy yourself. Be good to yourself.

"When we allow ourselves to wallow in the big questions, we fail to find the small answers."

JULIA CAMERON

We need to live in the day, in the here and now. What can I do today towards my dream, my goals? Do that thing. Do what you can today with what you have today. Make the best of where you are today. Today is the day we are alive. If this was the last day of your life, what would you do?
It is good to make plans. It is good to build castles in the air. Today is today, start with the smallest thing you can do towards your dreams and do it.

God is in the present, God is in the now. Sit still and wait upon the presence of the Lord. Today is the day you are alive. If your mind is in turmoil, sit still and wait upon the presence of the Lord. Bring yourself into the present. Look around you. Listen to all the sounds. Become aware of your breathing. Call on God your Creator. Close your eyes and listen. Breathe in and out, in and out.

"We invoke the Great Creator when we invoke our own creativity, and that creative force has the power to alter lives, fulfill destinies, answer our dreams."

JULIA CAMERON

I would call the great Creator, the Creator of heaven and earth, of people and all the natural order of things. Everyone has their own beliefs. Everyone has their own understanding of life and creation, of good and evil, of existence and the after life. Whatever our beliefs, life exists, we are here, the earth exists and all plant and animal life exists and we have all been set in motion. The sun rises and the sun sets day after day. There is air around us to breathe and water to drink. To be alive is a gift, a gift from some source. I call that source God.

When we open ourselves to our creativity, we open ourselves to God's power flowing through us, we open ourselves to all the unseen forces for good in existence.

Destruction is the antithesis of creation. The forces of destruction are diametrically opposed to those of creation. I believe that these are evil. When we open ourselves to these dark forces we destroy ourselves little by little. We destroy ourselves, our relationships, our homes, our communities and our country.

There is no vacuum in nature. At every given moment in our day and in our lives we are either serving the forces of creation or the forces of destruction.

"COVENT GARDEN"

WEEK 34

"The first place to look for a solution is within the problem itself."

BEN MEZRICH

"The antidote for shame is self-love and self-praise."
                                        JULIA CAMERON

What is shame? Shame is taking on other people's guilt for what they have said or done. It is feeling sick and disgusted with yourself. It is feeling responsible for other people's behaviour. It is feeling in the wrong, when you are not. Accepting guilt and blame for things you did not do, but were done to you. True guilt is for the things you did or did not do which were wrong.

What is self-love? It is to love yourself, to be good to yourself, to be kind to yourself. It is to stop berating yourself or chastising yourself or blaming yourself, for what you or other people say or do. It is to treat your body with respect, to be kind to your mind, to surround yourself with supportive friends. It is to relieve stress from your life as much as possible. It is to give yourself play time, fun time and leisure time. It is to give your body good quality food to eat, health care and dental care. It is to give yourself fresh air and exercise, entertainment and good company. It is to dress as well as you can, and remove yourself from toxic company. It is to give generously and receive graciously all the gifts and help you are offered. It is to stop when things get painful.

Praise yourself out loud, in writing and in your mind. Award yourself a certificate. Post yourself a well done card. Buy yourself some flowers. Take a bow, take a bow. Well done. Well done. Well done you!

"Pointed criticism; if accurate, often gives the artist and inner sense of relief."

JULIA CAMERON

This is the only healthy form of criticism which is of one's work, one's actions or one's thoughts and gives insight into a flaw in one's work or actions. Most criticisms are derogatory and seek to degrade and put down the person receiving them. Self criticism can be very destructive. "Why did I do that?" "What a stupid thing to say." "I am so dense." "I am no good." "I am a moron." "I am so lazy." "Why can't I do that?" "I look awful." "Nobody likes me." "I am ugly". "I am fat." "I am scrawny."

Once you become aware of your inner critic, stop it. Change the record. Replace the negative with a positive and repeat it over and over to yourself, out loud or in writing. "I am a good person." "I deserve love and respect." "I love and respect myself." "I have a beautiful body." "I have an excellent mind." "I am a very talented person." "I am smart." "I am very fit and healthy." "I have plenty." "The world is full of plenty." "God's supply is inexhaustible." "Abundance is available to me in the world." "My eyesight is perfect." "I am beautiful." "I am handsome." "I am strong." "I have constant clarity." "God is with me all the time." "I am in God's perfect care at all times." "I am unique." "There is no one like me." "The very best of what life has to offer is available to me." "All is well." "I am a well person." "I always make good decisions quickly." "I am surrounded by love and affection."

"Looking back, it was a set up to begin with. They want you. You want the job. But to do it well is to lose it."
NICOLS KRAUS & EMMA MC LAUGHLIN

It is the same with parenting, just on a longer time frame. If you do a good job they leave you, at first for short periods, then longer periods and eventually they become fully independent. Letting go is painful. Letting go of control, of wanting things to go your way, of wanting a specific person to love you or a specific house, job or material possession, is a challenge. The more you let go the more freely you flow. Life is an exercise in standing still and letting go. Wisdom is knowing when to stand firm and when to let go.

There is a right time for everything. There is a time to stand firm and a time to let go. Guidance for this comes when you stay close to God. When you stay close to God, your repressed feelings get vented healthily and your mind clears. With a clear mind you can see yourself as you are and the situation you find yourself in as it is. In a strange way you create the situation you are in. So stand still and look at what is happening, inside you and outside you. Look at yourself first. Is there a repeating pattern here? Why? What is really going on here for you? God is with you, oh so gently. Open your mind. What is really going on here for you?

"We address the fact that creativity requires receptivity and profound trust."

JULIA CAMERON

To be receptive is to be open-minded, to be open to receive, to be open to guidance, inspiration and contact with the power of good outside and inside of yourself. It means to be open to the well-spring of creation and all creative forces. It means to have our inner ear open to promptings from a positive spiritual source. It means to be tuned into the universal good. It means to be open to promptings of a positive nature from beyond the pale.

Trust. Trust is wonderful and frightening. It is letting go absolutely. In order for you body to float, you need to surrender completely to the water. In order for your spirit to float, you need to surrender your entire self to the force of good in the world. Let go of all negativity, all fear, all resentments, all buried anger, grief and losses. Let it all go. Let it go completely. Allow yourself to surrender totally to the universe of all good, all love, all support, all kindness and all healing. You are in a warm bubble of love and healing. You totally deserve to be there.

"My children, count the days of conquest as very blessed days."
TWO LISTENERS

We are all part of a great spiritual battle which stretches back in time to the origins of mankind. We are all part of the battle between good and evil. It is played out within us and between us and around us. Whose side are you on? Whose side do you want to be on? There is no vacuum on the natural or the supernatural plane. At every moment of every day of your life you are either serving good or evil. There is no in between. Your first responsibility is to yourself. Surrender yourself to the care of God or good orderly direction. The more you surrender of yourself and your will, the more your life will evolve into what it was meant to be. Before the resurrection comes the crucifixion. We need to go through the cross into the resurrection. We need to surrender all our past. We need to surrender all our current addictions, compulsions, obsessions and all our crutches one by one. We need to let go of all the toxins: fear, buried anger, resentment, guilt, shame, self loathing, wrong thinking, escapism, attachments to false dreams and ideas. Stand naked before God.

"Learn, first that I know what loneliness, desertion and solitude mean. Learn that every act of yours of faithfulness is a comfort to my Heart."

TWO LISTENERS

We all have lessons to learn. The quicker we learn them the easier our life will be. If we do not learn our lessons they will be repeated over and over again in our lives. Do you have a repeated pattern of some destructive kind? Do you repeatedly find yourself in financial difficulties? Do you repeatedly find yourself in toxic relationships with the opposite sex? Do you find yourself repeatedly falling out with your friends? Is your health constantly breaking down? Do you go from one dead end job to another? Then you are repeating some destructive pattern and there is some lesson you need to learn. It is your problem, no one else's. Stop blaming. Take full responsibility for the condition of your own life. Stand back from your life, have a good look and identify your pattern. Use what ever means you can to stand back from your life. Go on a retreat, a workshop or therapy weekend, or a long walk into the country. Join a self-help group, go for personal counselling or follow the tasks of a personal development manual. Whatever means comes to hand use it. We are put on this earth to learn and to grow spiritually and to help other people along the way. Keep an open mind.

"HAVEN DESCENDS"

WEEK 35

"Who said you had to answer your phone just because it rings? Free yourself from this distraction. Give yourself the gift of silence – it can be a great new source of energy."

CHERYL RICHARDSON

"I lead a life of sacrifice and work."

THE FATHER

There are good sacrifices and bad sacrifices. Good sacrifices are when you sacrifice something for your own or someone else's greater good. It is a good sacrifice to give up or let go of things that are addictive for you like, alcohol, sugar or drugs. Letting a child go for adoption, when you know that is the best chance they have of a decent life, is a huge sacrifice but a good one. Letting go of a marriage or a relationship that has become destructive and unredeemable, is another big sacrifice but good.

Bad sacrifices are giving people what they want just to please them. Bad sacrifices are taking responsibility for other adult's lives or finances. Their lives may seem to be in a mess and they may want you to take over, but their lives and finances are their own responsibility, not yours. Another bad sacrifice is where you give up your own truth in order to conform to some ideal forcing yourself into a mold that is not right for you. Giving time, money or goods that you need for yourself or your family is a bad sacrifice. Give from your excess and be generous. God is with you all the time.

"They ripple tensely, they can hardly contain their happiness......
They bow shyly as wet swans.
They love each other.
There is no loneliness like theirs."

JAMES WRIGHT

I am not alone. I have never been alone. God is always with me. God is always with us. It is we who turn away from him or tune him out. We have free will. We can choose our actions, our thoughts and our reactions to others all the time. God will not stop us doing what we want to do. If we put ourselves into God's care or someone else puts us in God's care then everything that happens to us is for our ultimate good or some one else's. It is sometimes hard to feel it, know it or believe it. It is wonderful when we get an experience of the presence of God. It gives us a huge boost of spiritual energy. Catholics have the bonus of being able to sit in the presence of the Blessed Sacrament, soaking up the presence of God. But the Spirit of God is everywhere. Just ask for it. Ask for it to come to you. When two of three people ask for it, it is stronger. You will get it if you ask for it. Like a nagging child, if you keep on asking for something you will get it eventually. Keep on asking God for his Spirit and it will descend upon you or explode in you. It will come. Ask now. Ask often.

"All the times your father treated you mean. Our Lady was the voice in you that said, 'No I will not bow down to this. I am Lily Melissa Owens, I will not bow down.' Whether you could hear this voice or not, she was in there saying it."

SUE MONK KIDD

"I will not bow down." No, we do not have to bow down to anything that puts us down, to anything that deprives us of human dignity and the right to a decent life. No I will not bow down to being beaten or assaulted in any way. No, I will not bow down to verbal abuse or sarcastic comment. No, I will not bow down to being berated, criticized, put down, ignored or mistreated in any way. I deserve all the best that life has to offer and more. I deserve a good life with love and caring. I deserve to be treated with respect and dignity. I deserve fresh air, clean water, shelter, food and decent clothing. I deserve rest, recreation and care for my body. I deserve the best, the very best that life has to offer and I accept nothing less. All is well. All is well.

"This is the time of graces, foreseen and awaited since the beginning of time! I am here personally to talk to you. I have come as the most tender and loving of fathers."

THE FATHER

Grace is a mysterious thing. It is a gift from God. It is the power of God working in us and about us. It is unmerited, we do not deserve it, nor can we work for it. It just comes. Suddenly God is doing for us what we cannot do for ourselves. Clarity and strength arrive in a moment. A weight is lifted off us in an instant. It is a most marvellous and wonderful thing. Perhaps at some time in the past we asked God for it and then let go of wanting it desperately. It never seems to come when we are desperate. Maybe some one else asked on our behalf. But when it happens, it is wonderful. We are like drooping plants that suddenly get water. We are rejuvenated. All negativity is banished. All disordered passions quieted. Truth and clarity abound. All obsessions and compulsions lifted. Wonder, truth, clarity and strength abound.

"No coward soul is mine.
No trembler in the world's storm – troubled sphere!
I see Heaven's glories shine,
And Faith shines equal, arming me from Fear."

EMILY DICKINSON

Take a risk. Go forward bravely into the future. Follow your dreams. Go where you have never been before. Do the thing you have been putting off for days or years. What is it you really want to do? Take one little step towards it today. What is the dearest wish of your heart? Write it down. What do you need to do to accomplish it? Write it down. Start with the smallest action you can take in that direction. Write out an action plan. Start at the beginning. Do it today. Your dreams are from God. God is with you in fulfilling them. Do not be afraid. God will hold your hand and together you will do it. Start today. Buy a note book. Start by writing down your dreams. Action is the magic word. Do some action everyday towards your dream, some small action. Do not be afraid. It is your destiny. Go for it. The doors will open as you take action. You must start. You must take the first step. Then God will take the second step. Go forward bravely into the future.

"Nothing is realistic or unrealistic, there is only what we think about any given situation. We create our own reality."

SUSAN JEFFERS

Look at everything that has happened in your life so far as positive and good. Bless all your life from the moment of your conception to this moment. Bless everything that has happened to you. All your pain will be released. All your wounds will be healed. All your lessons will be learned. We were not put on this earth to suffer. But pain comes. Bless it. Bless all the painful times and situations. It will be released and healed. It is not for us to hold on to pain and distress. Let it go, let it work through your body and be released into the stratosphere. Let it all go. You are loved. You are precious in God's eyes. Every hair on your head is counted. You are important, you are very important. Every moment in your life is valuable. You are like gold tested in a furnace. You are loved.

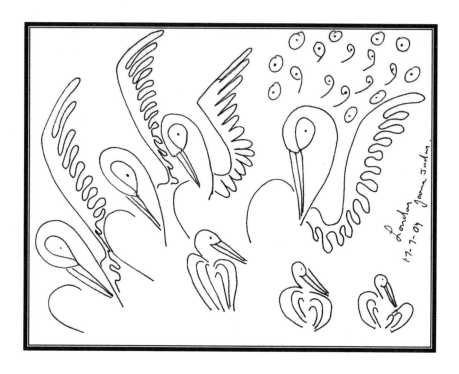

"PELICANS"

WEEK 36

"Problems are solved not by giving new information, but by arranging what we have known since long."

LUDWIG WITTGENSTEIN

"Our creative work is actually our creative self at play in the field of time. At the heart of this play is the mystery of joy."

JULIA CAMERON

Joy is wonderful. Joy is so rare nowadays. Life seems so complicated. Joy is so simple. In joy we live in the moment. The past is gone, the future is a mystery. Joy is full of hope, full of possibilities, full of positive expectations, full of wonder. Play is wonderful. Play brings you into the present. This is where God resides. God is in the now. In the present, the past can be healed and the future laid down. Now is the moment. Now is the moment to feel. Now is the moment to hear, to see, to smell and to touch. Look round you, what do you see? What do you hear? Is that the refrigerator humming? How do your clothes feel against your skin? Feel all over your body. What is pressing into you and where? How does your body feel? Do you have any pain? How is your neck? How are your eyes? Any strain there? Are you hungry or do you crave food? What emotions are you feeling? Feel them. All is well with the world. All is well now and forever more.

"Homeopathic remedies do not work directly on the body, but rather when the healing process is faulty, encourage the natural forces of the body to restore health and harmony."
SUSAN CURTIS, ROMY FRASER & IRENE KOHLER

Health and harmony go together. Wholeness is God's will for us: to be functioning well at all levels, physical, mental, emotional, financial and spiritual. We live in our body. Our body reflects our psyche. Our bodies hold our memories. All our blocked feelings and emotions are stored in our bodies. The areas of tension in our bodies tell the tale of our lives. You cannot work on your body effectively without working on your mind and spirit as well. Painful memories are stored in your body. Touch can release your memories. All forms of non-sexual massage can bring memories back. All parts of your body damaged by violence or sexual misuse store the memory of destructive events. Your body can be read like a book of your life. Your body is very precious. It is very precious in God's eyes. You were conceived, in God's mind, as a perfect functioning human being. Every cell in your body is precious. You are precious. Love yourself. Take care of your body. Be good to yourself. Be gentle with yourself today and every day.

"I realised that the reason I cared so much for Nancy was that she, like myself, was one of the Duke's children, one of those outcasts of a lost fatherland who go through life, living above and beyond themselves like some image of man's original aspiration."

FRANK O'CONNOR

How many of us are like this. We sense that there is a better life to be lived maybe somewhere else, maybe with someone else or maybe with a different job or career. We have a sense that life could be better. I believe it is possible. These feelings of displacement are real. We are not living the life we were meant to live. But the changes that are needed are inside us not outside. The outside will change after the inside. We start with our life as it is at present. We start today, now. What are all the good things of your present life? What are your dreams? Write down your dreams. What are the dearest wishes of your heart? What is stopping you from granting them to yourself? What can you do today towards the realisation of your dreams? Dreams are good. They are glimpses of heaven, your personal heaven on earth. The life you were meant to live. So go for it, follow your dreams. Start today, to build the foundations of your castles in the air.

"Listening to the siren's song of more, we are deaf to the still small voice waiting in our soul to whisper, 'you're enough'."

JULIA CAMERON

Do you have enough for today? Then you have enough. Look at all the good things in your life today. Really look at them. You are fortunate. You are alive. Who else that you care about is alive? You are blessed. Do you have contact with them? You are blessed. Do you have a place to sleep tonight? You are blessed. You can read. You are blessed. You have air to breathe. You are blessed. Can you see the sky, now or sometime during the day or night? You are blessed. Do you have someone to talk to today? You are blessed. Have you seen a bird today? A flower? You are blessed. Can you go for a walk, a run, a cycle, a swim, a ride on a horse today? You are blessed. Will you eat three meals today, two, one? You are blessed. Can you listen to or make music today? You are blessed. Do you have one friend anywhere in the world? You are blessed. Do you have some clothes to wear? You are blessed. Are you warm enough or cool enough? You are blessed. Your life is full of good things, look for them. God is talking to you all the time, pay attention. God talks through the song of birds, the rustle of leaves and the movement of clouds. Listen. Listen to him. He is there surrounding you with love and attention all the time.

285

"I have had frequent recourse to him and have opened up to him all the wounds of my soul without any reticence or fear."

PADRE PIO OF PIETRELCINA

It is good to have some body or bodies to reveal your inner self to, to open up your wounds to. They cannot be healed until they are opened and then drained away. For this you need trust and absolute privacy. Sometimes it is enough to do it on paper. That is, to write down all you feel about something or all you can remember about a wounding incident. This can help greatly. But there comes a time when the wound needs to be exposed to another human being. For this safety, security and absolute privacy comes first. The time will come and the place will come for this. Trust God. Trust God. All is well. All is well. All is very well.

"Take a bite out of this bitsy but beefy package, brimming with flavorized morsels of wit, wisdom and worldly knowledge."
                                        MATT GROENING

Are you "brimming with flavorized morsels of wit, wisdom and worldly knowledge"? We all have some "worldly knowledge", or else we could not survive in this world. Some people can surrender to mental illness or physical illness and have other people take full responsibility for them. Others give up on life and opt for suicide. Do not surrender to these, surrender to life. Surrendering to life is very challenging. It is easier to stay put than to change, to go forward. Staying stuck is easy. It is easier to stay in a destructive relationship than to get out of it or challenge it. To change you must stop doing the destructive things you are doing. Stop thinking in destructive ways, stop all compulsions, addictions and obsessions. Ask for help. Ask God, your Creator, for help, your own inner guide. Deep inside of you, you know what is good for you. The still small voice is there. The stray image shows you, your dream life. Go for it. Go for truth, health, wisdom and abundant life. Go for it. Dare to change. Dare to live life to the fullest.

"D"

WEEK 37

"The heart of another is a dark forest, and as the twilight ebbed past I watched him silently walk away, becoming a dark speck, until finally I lost him."

NORMAN SHERRY

"So your behavior was your testimony of truth."
HARVEY GILLMAN

Ultimately, what you do matters. All changes on the inside are reflected on the outside. Once you have surrendered your whole life and all its aspects to God, the creative force of all good, you will start to change. These changes will eventually become apparent on the outside. Your behaviour will change. You will be challenged to make changes in your life, both small and big changes. Work on the small changes first before you make the big leap. Once you are in contact with your Creator, you can not stay in toxic situations for long. It is not the Creator's will that you or those you are responsible for, be used or abused in any way. The natural order is towards health, longevity, wholeness and total well-being. Toxic situations destroy your spirit and your body. Be gentle with yourself. Go forward slowly. Keep going forward. There is light at the end of the tunnel. Keep going forward.

"I began to realize that my God had been appearing to me in human beings that I had been forced to ask for help."

ANONYMOUS

God can work in all sorts of ways. He can communicate to us though many channels. His love for us can come to us through other people. Every good, gentle and positive thing ever done for us has come from God through them. It is his way of saying, "I care for you", "You are special to me", "I love you".

"The key here is action. Pain that is not used profitably quickly solidifies into a leaden heart, which makes any action difficult."
JULIA CAMERON

The way back from indecision and inactivity is action, small actions, small steps. What do you want to achieve? Write it down. What can you do today to start this process? What small step can you take today towards achieving your dream? Do it. Sometimes God talks to us through closed doors. It could be that it is not the right way for you to go, or it could be that it is not the right time. There are other options. To do nothing about that particular closed door is an option. There are other options to explore or maybe this is the time to relax, to regroup or to take a holiday. If money were no object what would you do? Do it. Start today. Make a commitment to that plan. The money will come. The help you need to achieve it will come. Money is God in action. Take the action and God will be with you.

"What specifically are you to be aware of? Your reactions and your relationships."

ANTHONY DE MELLO

According to Anthony De Mello, awareness is the key to happiness. Yes we do need to be aware of our reactions to other people, of the situations we find ourselves in, and of nature itself. In order to be aware of your reactions to other people you need to stand back to observe yourself, your behaviour, your thoughts and your feelings. What are my feelings towards that person or that situation? What is happening to me? To know yourself, you must observe yourself in every situation and every interaction with another human being. If you are not aware of yourself you are not in control of yourself. Other people are pulling the strings. You are in their control. If you have complete control of yourself you can control your world. In order to get complete control of yourself you need to surrender yourself to God your Creator. Then little by little, you see yourself clearly and gain more and more control over yourself and your life. If you are going down a path that is wrong for you, the door will not open. You will not prosper no matter how much effort you put into it. If you are on the right path, persistent effort is required but eventually the doors will open and success will be yours.

"All you need to do to receive guidance is to ask for it and then listen."

SANAYA ROMAN

God can speak to us in many ways. He can speak to us directly as an inner knowing or an actual word spoken. He can speak to us through books, TV, conversations with others, overheard conversations or commercials. He can speak to us through any channel of communication. The same word can come up again and again in our daily lives from different sources. The same suggestion can come up from several different people. That is God calling, God telling us the way to go. Guidance can come simply as an idea that pops into our head, or an idea that keeps coming back to you. That is God prompting you to go in a certain direction. We have free will, we can choose what to do or not do. We can choose how to think and how to react. There are certain jobs God wants us to do for him if we are willing to do his will for us. Most of his jobs are small ones and all are doable with his help. He might want you to call and see a friend, or phone a friend at a certain time. When people pop into my head I usually contact them. It has often turned out that, that person needed to hear something I had to say at that time. God's timing is perfect. The more we surrender our will to God, the more he can use us for the greater good of ourselves and others. God is with us to the extent that we let him be.

"Think of yourself as an incandescent power, illuminated and perhaps forever talked to by God and his messengers."

BRENDA UELAND

Yes, this is the truth. It is all there for us for the asking. All the light we need, all the help we need. Just ask for it. God wants us to have perfection, his perfection for us. He wants us to be the perfect functioning person he conceived us to be. That is his will for us. No one knows who this person really is but God and ourselves. He wants us to be perfectly happy, to perfectly live in accordance with his will for us. He wants us to have perfect poise, not to be disturbed or controlled by any force other than his will for us. We have free will all the time. We can freely choose his way or our own way or other people's way for us. So many people want to control us: the government, society, our friends, neighbours, relatives and lovers. But in a strange way, the more we surrender to God our Creator the more we gain control of ourselves and the more we become aware of others' attempts to control us. We also gain freedom from internal controls of addictions, obsessions and compulsions. The more we surrender to God the clearer our vision of ourselves becomes, and in seeing ourselves clearly we stop doing the things that damage us. We break our destructive patterns of behaviour. God wishes us to have life, abundant life now and for evermore.

"REFLECTIONS"

WEEK 38

"He rubbed a hand over his face. He felt exhausted and still slightly drunk; heavy with fatigue and self-disgust. The dream dragged at his spirits. Wrong doing and loss, he thought. Is that all there is?"

MICHELLE PAVER

"Creativity is oxygen for our souls."

JULIA CAMERON

Creativity is our own individual response to the world. If we stop being creative we stop being ourselves; our best selves. We all need some outlet to express our creativity. It does not have to be in the arts or entertainment aspects of life. We can express ourselves in our clothes, our homes, our gardens, our cars, our bicycles, in our cooking, our correspondence, our hair or our children. Do not be afraid to be yourself, to try new things out. Stagnation and total conformity are not good for our souls. We are unique individuals. We are special in God's eyes. God is never boring. Look at the sky. It changes all the time.

There are certain constants. Night and day is constant. The earth revolving around the sun is constant. The constants are the basis of life. Without this total chaos would ensue.

But variety is the spice of life. The fact that every time you make a stew it turns out differently makes life interesting. People change all the time. We change in our appearance and in our souls. No two snowflakes are the same. No two sunrises are the same. Variety in constancy is nature's way. To have a good life, we need to reflect this. Take a risk, a small risk today. Do something different. Get up earlier. Greet the sunrise. Take a different route to work. Buy some flowers. Switch off the TV. Leave down the book. Look around you. No two days are ever the same. Look, listen, smell, touch, feel and luxuriate.

"Shoot for the moon. Even if you miss it you will land among the stars."

LES BROWN

There is great power in action. There is always a response to action. Take a risk. Take a little risk today. Is there anything you always wanted to do? Make a list of all the things you would like to do and have never done. Pick one thing and start on the road to doing it. Launch out into the deep. Have a go. Try it. Do something different today. Make a small change. Look at the moon tonight. Look at the stars. God is in his heaven and all's well with the world. What is your personal moon? What is the dearest wish of your heart? Make a small step towards it today. Do it. God is with you – victory to the brave, victory to the brave.

"The unconscious wants truth. It ceases to speak to those who want something else more than truth."

ADRIENNE RICH

Deep down we all need to know our own truth. We need to know what happened to us as children, as adults. What made us the way we are today? Why did I do that? What are all the influences operating upon me now? What do I need to do next? You will always get answers to you own truth. Why did he/she do that? That is none of our business. Why did I react to him/her in that way? That answer will come to me in time.

We instantly know when we have hit the nail on the head. We recognise the truth when we are exposed to it. When you have a light bulb moment, write it down. That will help you to remember it. We can be so easily distracted and confused afterwards. It is always good to write down our bright ideas or insights. We need to know the truth of our existence. This will come if you ask for it and act on the guidance given. "Seek and you will find". You will find the answers to questions you need to know and have a right to know. Action and patience, all will be revealed in time, in God's own perfect time.

"Lord may you be blessed. For it is thus and it is good. And now we truly see that all is done as it was ordained before anything was made."

JULIAN OF NORWICH

I think what this is getting at is acceptance. To accept things as they are today now. Accept what happens to us and the current circumstances of our lives. We can work to change them but for today, accept everything just as it is. Just for today we are where we are meant to be. Just for today people are the way they are. Just for today accept everything as a gift from God.

Thank God for everything. Thank God for every red light, for every long queue and for every harsh word. Bless everyone who crossed your path. They are there for a reason. They are there to teach you a lesson, especially the difficult or painful interactions. Bless everyone in your life today. Tomorrow they may melt away. Just for today they are there and there for a purpose. Sometimes the purpose is to stand up to them, some times it is to say no, to them. Whatever the purpose, there is one. It was "ordained before anything was made". Trust God. Thank and praise God for everything. Try it for an hour. Try it for a day. Try it and see what happens.

QUESTION: "How do I know that I am precious?"

ANSWER: It is very hard to know. There is a strong life force; a will to live that has never been extinguished in me. There is a spirit that will not give up, a force keeping me alive. Several times I nearly died but it did not happen. There is some unknown force protecting me. Some force keeping me alive. It is hard to see my own value. I need to be reassured that I am valuable and loveable. It is great when I get it from other people. When it is not coming from others I can tell myself I am valuable and loveable, write positive things about myself, say positive things about myself, or look at the good I have done and rejoice. The more I see other people as precious, the more they will see me as precious and vice versa.

How do I know you are precious? I do not know. But there is a common thread running through humanity. If God loves me then God loves you also. If there is an element of divine presence in me, it is in you also.

Let God your Creator, love you and protect you. Let him do it. Let the love flow freely. Let it flow into your soul. Let it flow like a river; a river of love, a river of power; transforming power. God really loves you. Let him love you. Let him bring the right people into your life. Just let it happen. Bless yourself. Bless everybody. Bless everything that has happened to you. Bless everything that is happening to you. All is love. All is love. All is well. All is very well.

Come near me now
breathing lonely to my breast
When light softly vanishes on the bow
or on the rims of a nest.

JAMES KELLY

We all need contact. We all need touch. Babies thrive on it. Babies could spend their entire day in contact with their mothers or someone else's flesh. The most soothing thing to do for another person is to stroke them, stroke their head, their face, their hand, their arm or their back. It communicates so much more than words. "You are fine", "All is well", "Relax". We need touch to know we are alive, to know that we are accepted, valued and cherished.

Touch can be painful. A little pain, a firm touch can say: "Stop, do not go there". Other touch can be very painful and violent. It says, "You are bad", "I hate you", "Get away from me". Touch can communicate to us on a deeper, surer, truer level. Touch does not lie. To be untouched is to be lonely and isolated. To touch another human being is to connect to the human race. Touch is so necessary that if we do not get it in healing good ways, we can settle for violence or undignified sexual contact rather than none.

"Who touched me?" LUKE 8:45

"CITY GUARDIANS"

WEEK 39

"How many lives lost demands the declaration of war? ...Tens of thousands of lives are lost on the nation's roads each year and thousands more are murdered in our cities and towns. Is that too many? Can we 'tolerate' those deaths which we understand. However, we can neither understand nor tolerate having foreign terrorists attack and slaughter our citizens."

RICHARD L HOLM

"The darkness which envelops my soul is continually increasing, and far from perceiving the dawn the poor thing sees nothing but advancing night."

PADRE PIO OF PIETRELCINA

The dark night of the soul; it is very difficult in the midst of sorrow and darkness to come out of it. It can be all powerful and all consuming. Fear, doubt or sorrow takes over. What can help? Ask someone to pray for you. Pray for yourself. Ask God, the God of your own understanding, to take you out of it. Sometimes it can happen in an instant: puff and it is all gone. Bring your mind into the present. Look around you. Listen to all the sounds. Look at everything with fresh eyes. Switch off all distractions: TV, radio, music, computers, books, papers and magazines. Be where you are now. Feel your body.

Do simple practical things. Go for a walk. Wash the dishes. Sort out your sock drawer. Do your mending. Bring your mind to the task at hand. Do some baking, gardening, cooking. Go for a walk, a cycle, a swim or a run. Rhythmical exercise acts as a meditation. It calms the mind and brings you into your body. Fear paralyzes the mind and the body. Get your body going. Keep it simple. Do something. Action is the key to success. Keep on going.

"Each painting has its own way of evolving. When the painting is finished the subject reveals itself."

WILLIAM BAZIOTES

So with life, your own life. It is not easy to see the point of it all or where we are going. But keep on going. Life reveals its own secrets in time. The reason for your existence will manifest in time; maybe not in your lifetime, but afterwards. What can we do but keep on going. Keep on getting up each morning and doing the best we can. Sometimes moments of clarity come. Write them down. Life is full of distractions. It is easy to be distracted by other people, by conflict, by ideals, by excessive desire for love, money, status, possessions or power. Anything we are addicted to, obsessed about or have a compulsion for is a distraction. Such addictions distract us from our true selves and from living the life we were meant to live. They distract us from facing our individual pain; all the pain we carry with us from childhood and from our family tree, all the pain of our lives to date. Face your pain and feel your pain. Loss is our biggest pain; loss of actual love or loss of love expected but never given. Be gentle with yourself. It will come. Rest, in God's arms. Rest.

"Act instead of reacting. Peace comes when we take charge of our lives. When a problem comes along don't be a victim who just reacts, face the problem assertively and act."
LYNDA FIELD

Face life as it is. Deal with life as it comes along. Look at life squarely and clearly. Do not hide. Do not run unless it is the time to run. There is a time for running and a time to stand. Problems come for a reason. There is a lesson to be learned in everything that happens to us. It is not haphazard. God is always giving us challenges, opportunities: opportunities to learn, opportunities to grow, opportunities to change. 'Face the music.' Deal with whatever comes up to deal with. There is magic in boldness. Sometimes the enemy disappears when you face it head on. Fear dissolves on contact. Face your fear look it in the eye. There is magic in boldness. Face it. Deal with it. Courage, courage, courage. All is well. All is well.

"'I trust my perceptions', is another powerful affirmation to use as we undergo shifts in identity, 'A stronger and clearer me is emerging.'"

JULIA CAMERON

Deep down we all know what is right for us. We know at all times and under all circumstances what we should best do for ourselves. But we do not listen to the still small voice within. We ignore it. We rationalize it or we deliberately turn away from it. Deep down we know when we are doing something that is wrong for us. It could be staying in a place, a job or a marriage with the intention of is bad for us and we ignore it. It takes a lot of courage to admit to ourselves or another human being that we are wrong. Either on the wrong path or have done something that is wrong.

Ask God for clarity. Use the affirmations above in the quotation, by saying them over and over again and or writing them down over and over again. An affirmation is a positive statement about yourself in the present tense. It is really good to get rid of negative beliefs. Once you identify a negative core belief, apply a positive affirmation to counter it. If you believe in lack (that there is not enough money, time, space in the world for you) then you need affirmations about plenty. "There is plenty in the world for me." "All my needs are being met." "All I need is there for me." "I have plenty, plenty, plenty." "There is a plentiful supply always available for me." "Avalanches of plenty are coming to me now." Keep up the good work. The hardest part of the climb is just before the crest of the hill. Soon you will be freewheeling downhill. Keep on going.

"Those undeserved joys which come uncalled and make us more pleased then grateful are (the ones) that sing."

HENRY DAVID THOREAU

"Joy". How do you get it? You already have it. Joy comes from God. The closer I get to God the more I feel. The more I feel all of life's hurts and wounds the quicker I get to joy. Joy comes in the morning after a long night of pain. Joy is freedom: freedom from pain, freedom from guilt, freedom from anxiety, freedom from interior conflict, freedom from lies and freedom from false beliefs. Young children are naturally joyous. It takes a lot to rob them of their joy. Joy is our natural state. Take all the rubbish away and we are joyful, calm and alert. Take all the confusion, obsessions, addictions and pain away and we are joyful. Let go of all attachments. Live in the present. Be alive to the now. Joy is in the moment. Joy is in the present. Joy is living life as it is. All is good. All is good. All is well.

"Here in this body are the sacred rivers: here are the sun and the moon as well as all the pilgrimage places. I have not encountered another temple as blissful as my own body."

SARAHA

We live in our bodies. Some believe we choose our bodies before our conception. We are certainly responsible for them. All our memories are stored in our bodies. All the pain, neglect and abuse we have received in our lives is stored in our bodies. We need to be gentle with ourselves. We need touch, positive gentle touch, firm supportive touch. If we do not have plenty of good touch in our lives we can supplement it with non-sexual massage and immersion in warm water. Good touch tells us that we are important, we are precious, we are alive and we are wanted. Touch does not have to be sexual; though it can be, of course. We can live on a daily basis without sexual contact but we cannot live well without touch. Contact with some pet animals is so good for us, as they crave our touch and ask for it. Good touch is full of reassurance, full of love. Bad touch communicates hatred, contempt, condescension, anger and control.

Human beings need other human beings, we are social animals. We were not meant to live in total isolation. Touch is so powerful. It says "I am here for you", "I am with you." God has no hands and feet. We need to be God's hands and feet for each other.

311

"ALETHEA"

WEEK 40

"A flood of words is never without fault;
whoever controls the lips is wise."

PROVERBS 10:19

"When we try to control those we love we stand the chance of crippling ourselves and our loved ones."
EARNIE LARSEN & CAROL LARSEN HEGARTY

We can only let others be their best selves when we concentrate on being our best selves. If you are living a full life and looking after yourself and your needs, then there is no pull to control or manipulate others. We can be obvious controllers: giving orders, telling others what to do when it is not our place to do so; or subtle controllers: hinting, subtly making suggestions, knowing in your own mind what is right for others, fantasizing about what "should be". All forms of inappropriate controlling of other people is a waste of energy. Our energy is given to us firstly to maintain our own lives then to reproduce when the conditions are right. When you are well and being the person you are meant to be you automatically help others and do not try to control or manipulate them.

"Do not magnify obstacles, magnify the Lord – that is God's power. 'You combine with what you notice', so if you give obstacles and hindrances your undivided attention, they grow more and more."

FLORENCE SCOVEL SHINN

Whatever you focus on grows. So focus on the good. Focus on the good in your life today. Focus on the good in everyone you deal with. See God's power working in your life. Write down three wishes. Three things you would love to happen to you, be specific. Date it and put the piece of paper away in a jar. In three months time open the jar and see what has happened in that time.

Make a list of all that you worried about in the past year. What happened? Did the worst happen? Did it work out? Be grateful for everything that worked out. What worked out in the most miraculous and amazing way? Write about it. Remember it. Learn from your mistakes and let it go. The next time you will do better. Let all the past go. Trust more. Learn. Listen more. Listen to the God within, your intuition. Ask for guidance and listen for the answer. All is well. All is well.

"Go placidly amid the noise and the haste, and remember what peace there may be in silence."

MAX EHRMANN

Everything you say is important. Whatever you say is forming your future. All nastiness and negativity that comes out of your mouth will boomerang back to hit you, when you least expect it. If you feel angry, release you anger in a healthy way. Let it work itself out in physical activity: cleaning, painting, weeding the garden, brisk walking, a murderous game of squash, a fast run or cycle or tearing up cardboard boxes. Let it pour out on to a page in stream of consciousness writing. Keep the focus on yourself. Your anger is in you and you alone.

Once you anger is spent, pray for clarity and take whatever action is needed in the circumstances. Anger is there for a reason. It shows you a boundary has been crossed. All true anger comes from this. You may be angry today because of something in the past. If you are angry today, is your anger appropriate or exaggerated? If it is exaggerated then, look to the past. What is really going on for you? What does today's circumstance remind you of? Who are you really angry with, the man in the shop or your father in the past?

All buried anger from the past needs to be expressed in a safe way. Healing is also needed, as underneath all old anger is hurt, woundedness, loss and disappointment. Drain all your anger. Feel all your feelings. All is well.

"By seeing clearly the perfect plan, we could redeem the world, with our inner eye seeing a world of peace and plenty and good will."

FLORENCE SCOVEL SHINN

God's will for us is perfection. He wants to give us perfect peace, perfect health, perfect love, perfect self-expression, perfect supply and perfect abundance. He does lean heavily on some people and allows them to share his burden. Sometimes to have perfect compassion we need to experience pain, our own pain. The pain that is ours to experience. No resistance. No denial. Face your pain and feel your pain. Therein lies freedom. Perfection is the end result. Perfect freedom, perfect understanding, perfect clarity and perfect love. "Perfect love casts out all fear." Love yourself, love God and love your neighbour. Everything works itself out in time or sometimes in the twinkling of an eye. Sometimes when you hit the nail on the head marvellous changes occur instantly. The door opens and wonderful things happen. God is good. God is good.

"Life has need of all the charm of word and sound, of color and craven stone that love can give it."

MAX EHRMANN

Life with out love is dead, completely dead. Love gives power and direction. Love gives protection and peace. Love gives healing and hope. Love creates. Love envelopes. Love enlightens. Love empowers. Love dissolves and dissipates all anger and aggression. Love is wonderful, wonderful, wonderful.

"Whether you think you can or whether you think you can't – you are right."

HENRY FORD

So think that you can be adventurous and live life to the full. Do not be afraid to experiment, to take risks, to make mistakes and learn from them. Do not be afraid to take a risk. Move out of your comfort zone. Do something different today. Is there something you always wanted to do? Start today. Take the first step towards it. Start writing today. Make a list of all you need to do in order to accomplish it. Start with the simplest, easiest thing and do that. Keep going back to the list or plan and keep working on it until your goal is accomplished. It will come to pass suddenly after a lot of activity.

Take a different route to work or school. Leave the car behind, take the bus or train or bicycle. Do something different. Change your outlook, change your desk around, add flowers to your life, bless everyone you see, bless everyone you think about, buy yourself a present. Do something different. There is hope. There is life. All is well. All is well.

"ARAB WOMAN"

WEEK 41

"I used to be against CCTV, but earlier this year my wife's handbag was stolen in a coffee shop and there was the culprit caught red-handed on camera. Then he tried to buy petrol with her credit card and there he was again, number plate and all. Fantastic! Obviously nothing was ever done to follow any of this up, trace his car or bring any charges, but you can't expect everything."

JOHN O'FARRELL

"It is not God who has abandoned the world, it is the world that has abandoned God."

JAMES KELLY

This is true. Abundance, protection and healing all come from God. Once you turn to God, you can ask for all you need for yourself, for those close to you, for your community, for your country and for the world as we know it, for the dead and for the future unborn. "Ask and you shall receive." You must ask first. I do believe that God wants only the best for us individually and collectively. When we ask for something sometimes we have to wait a long time for it, as the conditions are not right now. Sometimes it comes quickly and it is delightful. Once I was sitting in a train in a foreign country. I was the only foreigner in the carriage. All eyes turned to me. The atmosphere in the carriage turned hostile towards me. I started to pray for all the people in the carriage, all the people on the train and all the people in the country I was in. Suddenly all the hostility faded. It just melted away.

Pray about everything. All that is close to your heart, all the people you know, all the people you have had contact with in the day, all the people you have ever had contact with. Pray about everything and everyone. Prayer is like a laser beam, directing God's love and power in a specific direction unto a specific target. Once you turn to God, you are automatically protected as you are in his care now. Believe it. All is well.

"Awareness is a delight, the delight of a little child moving out in wonder to discover the world. For even when awareness brings unpleasant things in you, it always brings liberation and joy."

ANTHONY DE MELLO

Liberation and joy," these are the fruits of awareness. It is first of all awareness of yourself, your own actions and reactions to other people. Why did I do that? What is happening to me? Why am I reacting to this situation like this? What is really going on for me? These are good questions to ask? Our tendency is always to blame the other person or the situation we find ourselves in. What is wrong with them? Why did they do that? What can I do to change this situation? No. No. No. These are the wrong questions.

First, focus on yourself, on your actions and more importantly on your reactions to others. Once you see what you are really reacting to then the past influences and the present situation separates out. When you can, see the past clearly (in relation to the current situation), feel all unexpressed feelings, correct all misconceptions and old destructive thought patterns, then can you deal effectively with the present. When you are operating truly in the present you can see the current situation clearly, act wisely, enjoy all the good things, avoid all distractions and deflect all ill will.

"Pain. This is not an illness in itself, but a reaction to a physical or psychological cause, and it is that cause which one needs to identify and treat."

SUSAN CURTIS, ROMY FRASER & IRENE KOHLER

Pain comes as a warning. It says stop. Stop doing whatever you are doing that is causing it. It says you have gone too far, abused your body too much and ignored the signals of distress. Pain says stop. Something is wrong. If you ignore pain, whatever is causing it will get worse and worse. If you deaden pain the cause does not go away, it just gets worse and worse. Both physical pain and emotional pain are there for a reason.

Emotional pain is caused by some deep woundedness. This pain needs to be released when the conditions are right. Emotional pain is a wound in you soul, a wound in your psychic. Trust has been violated. Protection breached. The integrity of your heart, soul or body has been compromised. Emotional pain needs to be felt. This can only happen when you are in a safe place, surrounded by love.

Love heals. Allow yourself to feel the loss, the loss of trust, the loss of love, the loss of expectation, the loss of safety and the loss of physical integrity. Feel the pain, allow the wound to open, oh so slowly. All is well. All is well. Let the feelings come. It is OK to feel. Let the feeling come. Feelings will not kill you but keeping them buried might. Deeply buried resentment causes illness, possibly even cancer. So be good to yourself. Be gentle with yourself. All is well. All is well.

"So give your servant a heart to understand how to govern your people, how to discern between good and evil."
1 KINGS 3:9

Wisdom and discernment, what is it? It is the ability to see clearly and act effectively in every situation; it is the ability to understand and to know whatever is the right thing to do; to be able to see into your own or other people's hearts. This is a great gift. Solomon asked for this. He received this gift as well as riches, a long life and lots of wives and concubines. We can ask for what we need and what we would like. We can leave the fulfilling of the request up to God. Once I expressed a desire for an Alfa Romeo car. Six months later I needed to buy a car and up comes an Alfa at a very reasonable price! I had completely forgotten about my wish. Ask God for whatever you need, if you need clarity, money, health, companionship or love, ask for it. Always ask for what is perfect for you, the perfect friend, the perfect spouse, the perfect job, the perfect house or the perfect outfit. Perfection is always God's will for us if we are willing to accept it.

Do you believe that you deserve the absolute best? Well if you do and you ask for it, you will get it, in time and in a perfect way. Are you open to receiving the best of clarity, wisdom and understanding; the best of health, mental and physical; the best, most prosperous life; the best self-expression for you? Always ask for what is best for you and be open to receiving it. It will come in time in a perfect way.

"Be bold and bring back some of the country's produce."
                                        NUMBERS 13:20

"Be bold", be strong, be courageous, be audacious. Take risks, fear not, go forward unafraid. Step out into the light. Take a risk. Once you have handed over your life, your will and every situation you encounter into the care of God, you will be protected. The perfect result will happen every time you take a risk or leave your comfort zone. So do it. Go forward. Take the risk and the safety net will appear. Whatever happens will be the best result for you. It may not be what you expected or wanted to happen but it will be the best for you. So rejoice. Sometimes it is obvious that after taking a risk, the result is positive. Other times the result may appear negative, but it is not. A negative result or no result is the best for you in that circumstance. In time you may see that it was good. Sometimes you may not see the good in it, but it is there. God is with you all the time, protecting you and guiding you. So "be bold", today. Follow your hunches.

"Misfortune is due to failure to stick to the things which spirit has revealed through intuition."
                    FLORENCE SCOVEL SHINN

When you are unsure or uncertain about something, pray for clarity, pray for guidance. These prayers are always answered. Clarity will come. Guidance will come. When you have moments of clarity write it down. Then stick to the plan. Do not let yourself be deflected. Do not let the wet blankets or the doubting Thomases affect you. In fact, be very selective about who you share your ideas with. Big ideas, good ideas or new ideas always meet with opposition. Keep on going. Do not give up. Stick to positive people. Refer back to what you wrote down when you were very clear about the direction you should take.

Intuition is a hunch. Go with your hunches. These are from God. It is God giving you a little nudge in the right direction. Some people may refer to their hunches as their 'gut', or their 'guardian angel'. Whatever you call it listen to it and obey straight away. By all means obey straight away. All is well. All is well.

"LAMP IN PARK"

WEEK 42

"A kinless, lordless, friendless man or woman was as good as dead or worse, for even the dead had family and friends who remembered them in their prayers. Severance of social ties was so drastic that only the worst criminals suffered it and only the craziest ascetics accomplished it."

LISA M BITEL

"Be undisturbed by a situation and it will fall away of its own accord."

FLORENCE SCOVEL SHINN

What does it mean to "be undisturbed" by a situation? To be undisturbed by a situation means to accept it for what it is, it means to accept whatever the situation is now today, it means to let go of all strong emotional reactions to it. In order to be able to let go of them you need first to look at them. What am I thinking, feeling, as a result of this incident? Where are those thoughts and feelings coming from? To do this honestly you need to focus on yourself and your reactions, not on other people's actions. Keep the focus on yourself. What am I feeling now? Work through these feelings, track them to their source and then let go of them.

Today you are in this situation. This is what you have to deal with today. Now is the moment. God works in the now. He will give you clarity and insight whenever you ask for it. So ask for it now. Bless the situation, bless everyone in it and bless especially the person who seems to be causing it. Let go of all bitterness. Let go of all fear and all resentment, all anger towards this situation. It will fall away, it will dissolve into nothingness. All is well. All is well.

"So let us become Miracle Conscious and prepare for miracles, expect miracles. and we are then inviting them into our lives."

FLORENCE SCOVEL SHINN

One of the dictionary definitions of miracle is an 'amazing event'. So expect to be amazed! Expect wonderful things to happen. Enter again the world of wonder and joy that small children live in. Another definition of miracle is 'an act of God'. That is something that defies explanation. Expect miracles. Expect amazing things to happen. Live in the present. Look around you. Look at the sky. It is constantly changing. Search for flowers. Smell the flowers. Be where you are now. Expect perfect health, perfect supply of money and material goods, perfect love and perfectly satisfying activities and you will get them. Expect amazing events and they will happen. What amazing event happened in your life today? Yesterday? Think. There was at least one. What amazing events have happened in your life so far? Think, what stands out?

"Success is failure turned inside out
The silver tint of the clouds of doubt,
And you never can tell how close you are,
It may be near when it seem so far.....
You must not quit."

C W LONGENECKER

The darkest hour is before the dawn. It is the natural order to go down first before coming up. The powers of evil attack most virulently just as we are about to make a breakthrough. Evil works most through distraction, doubt and despair. We need spiritual help to keep going forward. Ask people to pray for you, to send you positive vibrations, to hold you in their thoughts, to do whatever they do to connect you to a positive spiritual source. I do believe it is the one source of all goodness, others may not do so. It does not matter so long as the connection is made. We need others to pray for us and with us. Alone we are vulnerable and our mind clouds. Every doubt or negative thought needs to be stamped out. For every negative thought there is an positive affirmation to replace it.

Two or more people together on the same spiritual path can achieve great things. Once they surrender themselves and their activities under the mighty hand of God, miracles happen. Do not quit on your spiritual path. You may let go of friendships, relationships, ideas, places or jobs. But stay on the path of your greatest good. It leads to your promised land of perfect supply, perfect love, perfect health and perfect self expression.

"Do not be afraid of poverty. Let money flow freely."

TWO LISTENERS

Do not hoard or hold on to money. Let it flow out freely with discretion. If you need something spend the money. Money freely flowing out will flow back again. Let God be your supply. All you ask for you will get, if you need it or want it and it is good for you. Feel rich. Do whatever you can to feel rich. Some people feel rich if they buy some fresh flowers, wear silk underwear, buy exotic fruit, wear perfume, take a bubble-bath, have comfortable socks, have a big cigar, have clean sheets or have a clean cloth handkerchief. Whatever makes you feel rich do it. It does not have to cost a lot. The more you give out the more will flow back in. Bless all bills and demands for money. Pay your bills with joy. Send out blessings with all the money you spend. Be generous to yourself. Treat yourself well. Make sure you have all you need to have a comfortable life and more. Spend your money wisely, putting first things first. Do not be mean to yourself or others. Take good care of your body. It is the only one you have. Love yourself. Treat yourself to all the good things available in your life today.

Do not hoard. If you do not need it, move it on. Let all rubbish go. Do not keep any junk. Clear out all unused items of clothing and personal property. Sell or give away all unnecessary possessions. Pass it on. When you pass it on, bless the receiver, bless the item. Send it out with love.

"And so when his accusers saw the honour done to him by this proclamation, and Jonathan himself invested in the purple, they all fled."

1 MACCABEES 10:64

This is about justification. Jonathan obeys God and did what was right for him. In time he was given the protection and respect he deserved. Then those who tried to bring him down fled. If we stand firm and continue to do what is right for ourselves, in time all negativity will fall away and we will be justified publicly. The battle is within. Keep on fighting the good fight. God is with you. Do you want to act in truth and justice? Do you want to see the truth and act with wisdom and fairness? Be true to yourself and all will work out in the end. Keep close to God, whatever your understanding of God may be, and you will more and more see the truth and act accordingly.

Once you start to move forward in the truth, your own truth, an army of aliens arise up against you. Fear, doubts, angers and resentments assail you. Keep on going. Do not give up. You are on the right path. God is with you. God is with you.

"It takes determination and eternal vigilance to check up on words and thoughts. Thoughts of fear, failure, resentment and ill will must be dissolved and dissipated."

FLORENCE SCOVEL SHINN

Why? Because thoughts of "fear, failure, resentment and ill will" bring those very things about. They boomerang out from you and bring back suspicion of actual failure, resentment for others and ill will towards you and your family.

A friend of mine once had a flat tyre. She was alone on a country road with a car full of small children. A man passed in a car and did not stop to help. She cursed him saying she hoped he would get four flat tyres himself. Within a month she herself got a further three flat tyres, four in all! Ill will and curses always comes back to you or your family tree. Unborn generations can be affected by your curses.

To dissolve and dissipate them you need to pray. Ask God to dissolve and dissipate all curses made by and on you and your family tree. That is, by all members of your family tree back seven generations and down to the present day.

Fear, failure, resentment and ill will can only be dissolved by God. Ask him to do it. Ask to replace fear with confidence in God, failure with success, resentment with compassion and ill will with love. Ask and you will receive. Once you ask for it you will get it as soon as and as much as you are ready for.

"TRAPEZE"

WEEK 43

"These Bloody days have broken my heart:
My lust, my youth did them depart,
and blind desire of estate."

SIR THOMAS WYATT

"We are always doing something, talking, reading, listening to the radio, planning what next. The mind is kept naggingly busy on some easy, unimportant external thing all day."

BRENDA UELAND

We need to stop this constant business at least once a day. Maybe you need to get up half an hour earlier or go to bed half an hour earlier or make use of your time on public transport. Stop doing, stop planning, stop listening and switch off the radio, the TV and the computer. Be with yourself. Be alert. Be where you are now. Feel your skin. What parts of your skin are exposed to the air? What does it feel like? Are your clothes tight anywhere? Are your clothes comfortable everywhere they touch your body? What do you hear? What do you see? Close your eyes. God is with you. God is surrounding you like warm air on a balmy night. Relax in his presence. You are completely safe now. You are completely safe. Your entire life from the moment of conception to this moment is in God's care. All the wounds of the past are being healed. Slowly but surely all is becoming well. All the wounds you inflicted on others are being healed. All the negative influences from past generations are being healed. All is becoming well. All is well. All is well.

"So there are two kinds of actions; some that do and others that do not depend on my will. And the mistake causing the contradiction is due only to the fact that I wrongly transfer the consciousness of freedom, ...to actions performed in conjunction with others and dependant on the coincidence of other wills with yours."

LEO TOLSTOY

I think what Tolstoy is saying here is that in reality we have very little free will, that our behaviour is influenced greatly by other people and the circumstances of our lives. Other people, current circumstances and past conditioning affect us greatly. True freedom for an individual or a nation is extremely rare.

In a strange kind of way the more we surrender our wills to God the greater the personal freedom we get. True freedom is about taking control of ourselves and making choices. Sometimes the choices prove good and sometimes bad. True freedom is about learning as you go, about taking risks and accepting the consequences. True freedom is about taking responsibility for your actions no matter what the extenuating circumstances are. You are responsible for your actions and inactions.

The more you surrender to God the more you see clearly, the more alive, alert and aware you become. The more aware you become the less likely you are to be influenced by the crowd or by any form of brainwashing or propaganda. Totalitarian regimes hate all religions they do not control, as they fear the influence on the minds of their subjects. The mind controls the body. If you want to control people's bodies you get at them through their minds.

"For neither can he clearly see his loving hand, who is most gentle and kind to him, nor can he see truly how he himself appears to his loving Lord."

JULIAN OF NORWICH

The "he", referred to here is man, or the Adam representing all of mankind and womankind. The "Lord", here is God. Julian saw a vision of God and man. Man had turned away from God, but God had not turned away from man. What, I think, she is saying here is that for the most part, we cannot see God clearly or understand how he sees us. This is our loss. God still loves us no matter what we have done or how little we understand or how far we are removed from his vision for us or how atrociously we have treated ourselves or others. God never stops loving us. We stop loving us. We stop loving ourselves and others. God still loves us. He still has a purpose for our lives. There is something you can do that no one else can do. It is something that appears too good to be true. It is something you personally enjoy and love doing. The seed is already placed in your mind and your heart. Ask to be shown it. Ask for a glimpse of it and it will come. Then go for it. Seize the day. Seize the day – victory to the brave.

"Friends have long tried to live out the importance of truth in every aspect of life. We can only be true to our innermost sense of spiritual harmony if we are faithful to the truth and honest in our dealings."

THE QUAKER TESTIMONIES

How difficult this is to live out, to be "true and honest in our dealings". That is with everybody, every organisation and every circumstance we deal with. Some times we shoot ourselves in the foot by talking too much, telling too much and giving too much information away. How much information are organisations entitled to gather? Has the right to privacy gone out the window completely? It seems that in the smallest transaction now we are being asked to part with a great deal of personal information.

Nowadays information is a valuable asset and personal privacy a rarity. We are perfectly entitled to protect our privacy as much as possible. We do not have to answer every question that is asked of us. We cannot control what other people do but we can control what we ourselves do. A lot of the information that is taken down, stored and used against us at a later date, is information that we volunteered initially. This we can control. We have control over our own behaviour and we have choices.

"He was selling his ethics, his standards, even his morals for money. Was his soul worth a million bucks? He took a sip of beer and washed away the fading twinges of guilt."

JOHN GRISHAM

This character in the book, "The Brethren", knew he was doing wrong. He did not have the courage to face it. So he drowned the still small voice, the voice of truth, with alcohol.

How many of us do that? Drown that voice of truth nagging, nagging away at us. We can drown it with alcohol, with sugar, with nicotine, with drugs, with work, with excessive exercise or with over spending, obsessive thinking or addictive sexual activity. It is still there, waiting to be heard. That nagging feeling that all is not well, that we are somewhat wrong, or on the wrong path, that something is missing. Whether there is outward prosperity or outward poverty it does not matter to the still small voice of truth. It is our own truth we need to face, the truth of our existence, the truth of our own personal histories, our truth no one else's. It does not go away. It is God knocking at the door of our consciousness. He will keep on knocking until we stop and listen, until we stop running away and turn to him for help, for strength, for guidance. He will show us ourselves, our relationships with others and our past, clearly. God is here, now, waiting. Turn to him.

"Our Lady was covered with hands, every shade of brown and black going in their own directions, but then the strangest thing started happening. Gradually all our hands fell into the same movement, sliding up and down the statue in long slow strokes, then changing to a sideways motion, like a flock of birds that shifts direction in the sky at the same moment, and you're left wondering who gave the order."

SUE MONK KIDD

Harmony. This is a description of perfect harmony. For that small space of time all the characters were united in one action. They were all going in the same direction at the same time. Any group of people, who get together for healing and growth, and who surrender themselves to God, reap great benefits and wonderful things happen to them. Two people together with a common purpose are more powerful than one, if they are united in their surrender to a higher power. God's law is perfect harmony. If there is disharmony, look first to yourself. Are you reacting to someone in the group? If so, bless that person and pray for that person. Keep it up until all bad feelings are dissolved and dissipated. Do you think the group itself is going astray? If so call a meeting and speak up. If there is something wrong the others will feel it too.

When perfect harmony exists God is giving the orders. Perfect harmony, perfect peace, perfect supply and perfect self-expression all come from God.

"FLOWERS"

WEEK 44

"If we strengthen our resolve, accept a degree of self-discipline, and embrace the new technologies, we will escape the trap of dependency and establish a secure, sustainable, and responsible energy system."

MICHAEL KLARE

"Force a hand, the voice warned, and it will fight you. But convince a mind to think as you want it to think, and you have an ally."

DAN BROWN

Thinking is a very powerful tool. Your mind is the most precious part of you. Your mind directs your body and your emotions.

There is huge competition nowadays for control of your mind. Every country and every society has its own form of political correctness. This is the way they want everyone to think. What is fashionable and acceptable today in thoughts or ideas could be out of favour in one year or ten years time. Vast sums of money are spent on planting in our minds that a certain idea, product or service is the best, the most acceptable, the most indispensable thing of its kind. In other words you must believe it, have it or use it to be safe, respectable or fulfilled.

Down through the ages different religions or sects have had a powerful effect on how people think. That is still the case today in many countries. People of power and influence know how important mind control is. If you want to control large numbers of people you do it through their minds.

Children's minds are first influenced by their parents, then the school and then the media. If you want to get directly at children's minds then you have to cut out or diminish the power and influence of their parents in their lives. The last century has brought a lot of pressure on the family and has undermined parental rights. By viewing children separately from their families you divide and conquer. This is not good for the children themselves, for their parents, for the community or for the country in the long run. Much prayer is needed in this area.

"Something deep inside us reacts to deception and betrayal. Betrayal not only inflames doubt and severs relationships with our neighbor, but also inevitably deepens hatred of ourselves."
                                        DAN B ALLENDER

The greatest betrayal of all is the betrayal of the sacred trust a child has in his or her natural parents. A parent, who does serious damage or stands by while someone else does serious damage to their child, is betraying a sacred trust. That is the trust God gave them at the child's conception. There is no job more valuable and important than rearing children well. It takes a lot of commitment and dedication to provide a stable, safe and secure environment for them to grow up into adulthood in. It is a 24-hour seven days a week commitment for at least 18 years! Parents need a lot of help and support. For the majority of people no other job has such far-reaching effects. Profound damage can be done to children growing up. A severely damaged child brings that woundedness into adulthood and can perpetuate it into the next generation. A child's heart is tender and his or her trust absolute. In a child's life every moment of every day is important. The parents' responsibility is awesome. Unless we heal and change ourselves we will pass our woundedness on to our children. They do not deserve it. As adults we are responsible for our own welfare and wellness. If you have any problems look for help. You deserve it and your children deserve it. God is always with us, but I believe he bends over backwards to help us when we want to treat our children well. All is well. All is well.

"Sunlight gleamed against the honey-house window, flickering now and then with a shifting cloud. We sat in the yellowish quiet for a while and worked without talking."

SUE MONK KIDD

Peace harmony and light. Only good things can take the light. All sin, ugliness, dirt, shame and guilt hides from the light. Once sin is exposed to the light it dissipates. Once we become truly aware of what we are doing and its effects on ourselves or others, we cannot continue to do it if it is wrong.
Why do housewives get a great desire to clean the house in spring? Because the light of the New Year shines brightly into their houses and shows up all the dirt of winter.

In the same way when the light of the truth is shone on our souls things change. Denial is a powerful negative tool. If we can deny that something terrible is happening, we do not have to do anything about it. But it nags away at the back of our minds and the pit of our stomachs. "Something is not right. Something is not right, pay attention." We continue to ignore it until something terrible happens which forces us to face it. Bless God for everything that happens. What appears to be a tragedy could be the very thing will bring us to a truth we needed to see. Once the truth is seen even for a little while, we can not go back to total denial and continue being sinful and destructive.

"'She is exactly, exactly like me, the very picture of me in every respect', the mother used to say to herself. 'Self – willed, horrid little imp! Nihilist, eccentric, mad and spiteful, spiteful, spiteful! Good Lord how unhappy she will be!'"

FYODOR DOSTOYEVSKY

The mother in this book, "The Idiot", knows and understands her daughter very well. She knows from her own experience that spite and self-will lead to unhappiness. Spite is speaking or acting out of hatefulness towards others. If you are not under grace, it will all come back to you. Self-will may get you control over other people or it may not, but it will always, always lead to exhaustion. You are trying to control people and events. This takes a great deal of energy, you may succeed but at what cost to yourself? Very often you are trying to force solutions, to your own or other people's problems. It may work for a while but it does not bring peace of heart or mind. It brings obsession, exhaustion, meanness, anger and frustration. Frustration always comes from trying to make things the way you want them to be. It also comes from too much self reliance. That is, believing that you, and only you can do it, that the outcome of every action depends on you.

You may get whatever you schemed and plotted for, but it will not bring you any lasting happiness. It may bring some fleeting pleasure and satisfaction which dissipates quickly. If it is not fulfilling your true destiny the happiness is short-lived and obsession will take over again.

The antidote to self-will is first acceptance then surrender. We accept things as they are for today, then, surrender our lives, our wills and the situation to God.

349

"'Grover', I say quietly, willing with all my heart, as if I were standing over my birthday cake, making the most important wish of my life. 'Just know that you are wonderful – fabulously wonderful and I hope somehow you'll know that I'll always be out here routing for you, okay?' I flick the last light off and scoop up the puppy."

NICOLA KRAUS & EMMA MCLAUGHLIN

Love is the most powerful thing. Yesterday as I was sitting in a train. A drunk man came and sat beside me. He put his hand on me and started to be verbally abusive to me. I started praying for him and blessing him, silently to myself. Suddenly his hand leaped off me as if he had been burned and he jumped up and started abusing others on the train as he left the carriage. I finally had no fear, I felt perfectly safe and I am perfectly safe.

Bless everybody. Bless everything that happens. Love is stronger than fear. Love and hate or love and fear can not abide together. The hatred and malice emanating from that man could not stay once I started blessing him.

The girl in the quotation had just been sacked from minding a little boy whom she had come to love. That kind of love never dies, it is always there. We will never know until the next world who really loved us and kept us in their hearts. I met a monk once who told me that he would keep me in his prayers all the remaining days of his life. What an amazing and wonderful gift! Even if he forgot me, God would remember and keep his promise for him.

All good things come through grace, which needs to be activated. Grace is something we need to ask for, for ourselves and others. It is God's power in action. It is like a laser gun, it needs to be powered up, aimed and fired.

"And then he went home and Veronica was in the kitchen and she did a fry for him, and he cried again when he was telling her about the pub and the match and meeting Jimmy Jr. And she called him an eejit. It was the best day of his life."

RODDY DOYLE

What makes for a good day? Is it perfection, harmony, well-being, joy and satisfaction? A day filled with positive actions, thoughts and feelings? May you, the reader, have many of these days. Sometimes we try to make special occasions into one of the best days of our lives, but the price can be very high, paid out in worry, anxiety and often a lot of money.

Then out of the blue a perfect day can come, no worry, no anxiety. There could be delightful surprises, pleasant company, pleasant surroundings or just a sense of well-being, a sense that all is well within and without. It could come after a job well done or a torment relieved. Perfect days do come. Perfect moments do happen. They come and they go. Open yourself to God and his universe. Pain will come and joy will come. The dawn will break through after the long night.

There are days of love, days of joy, days of peace, days of beauty, days of relief, days of justification, days of hope, days of satisfaction, days of gentle breezes and sweet smiles, days of soft tears, days of good company, days of delightful surprises and unexpected pleasures. Perfect days, perfect moments and perfect contentment do happen. Enjoy, enjoy. All is well. All is well.

"TABLE"

WEEK 45

"For the average... bureaucrat, time is not money, it is the interval between meals, between going to the office and leaving it, between the end of work on Friday and its start again on Monday."

JOE STUDWELL

"Jane was different. We'd get into a goddam movie or something, and right away we'd start holding hands, and we wouldn't quit until the movie is over... you never worried, with Jane whether your hand was sweaty or not. All you knew was, you were happy. You really were."

J D SALINGER

Connection. We so need to be connected to other people, whether there is an element of sexual attraction or not, it does not matter. People are social animals. We were not designed to live out our lives alone.

Touch is a most powerful means of connection. Touch can portray love and hate, anger and fear. Touch gives us a sense of our own bodies. Babies learn where their bodies end and the world begins, by being touched. Babies love being touched, firm touch, gentle touch, teasing touch and playful touch. They love it so much and respond so enthusiastically that older children and adults love to play with babies and hold them. Babies can give so much pleasure and draw out so much love from people. They are a gift from God. Their spirits are so pure. They have so recently come from God.

Adult sexual relationships return us to babyhood, for a time. If we have not healed from our childhood wounds, then a sexual relationship will bring us back to that woundedness again. Very often we need to give ourselves time to heal from childhood wounds first before we can have healthy sexual relationships.

"Queen: O Hamlet, speak no more
Thou turn'st mine eyes unto my very soul,
And there I see such black and grained spots as will not leave
their taint."

WILLIAM SHAKESPEARE

Facing reality is very painful. Looking at yourself, your past, what you did and did not do is very challenging. It is worth it. "The truth will set you free." That is, your own truth. In a strange way we need to see the worst things first, because guilt and shame drags us down. We need to see what was done to us that damaged us, what we did to others that damaged them and whatever we failed to do for ourselves or others. We need to see the things we are truly guilty of and also the guilt we carry, that we absorbed from other people's wrong-doing. Feeling guilty for other people's wrong-doing is shame. We need freedom from both guilt and shame. Our own guilt we need to acknowledge and make amends for. Shame we can let go of and return the guilt to its rightful owner.

Children can be blamed for their parents' or teachers' failures. They take this on board. "You are driving me to drink," a child is told and they believe it. Children are good at picking up the feelings that are flying around the atmosphere, but not at interpretating them or assessing the situation. This is how children absorb false beliefs about themselves. They believe what they are told and what is implied. Only as adults can the light of truth be shed on these false beliefs.

"The lesson I am working in now is to not have to prove myself to anyone. It's almost as if so much of what I have accomplished, I did to gain approval. I'd get more and more and it never seemed to be enough. The more I had, the more I wanted, and the more I feared losing what I had."

ANONYMOUS

We all have some core beliefs. The writer of this quotation believed that he, in his essential being was not enough. He believed that if he had enough he would be enough. This is a false belief. There was a hole in his soul that he tried to fill with money. It could never be filled. The harder he worked to fill it, the deeper it got.

Before we can change a negative core belief we first need to identify it. Stand back from your life and the situation you find yourself in. What are you doing in the situation? What are your thoughts and feelings about the situation? Look for repeating patterns. What situations are you coming up against again and again?

Many religions have a time honoured tradition of going on retreats. Retreats are times set apart from your ordinary life for prayer, reflection and possibly fasting. It is not only the nature of God we need to reflect on but our own nature, our own self. We are all a mixture of good and bad, positive and negative. As we keep turning back to God, the negative gets converted into positive. By taking time out we are helped to identify any negative behaviours and thinking patterns and root them out, make amends for past wrongs and replace negative core beliefs with true ones. "I am enough." "I have a perfect supply for every need." "God is with me." "God loves me unconditionally." "All is well."

"At eleven-fifteen, they walked through the front door of the administration building, the same door they'd each entered years ago, and waited on the hot sidewalk for their ride. None of them looked back."

JOHN GRISHAM

The day of their deliverance came. The door of their prison opened for them. It came suddenly and unexpectedly. Suddenly the three main characters of the book "The Brethren", were out. Sometimes change comes in the twinkling of an eye. The change comes first in us. We react differently, see things differently or see things clearly for the first time. Then a door opens, an opportunity presents itself and we are out; out of fear and doubt, out of uncertainty and poverty, out of illness and ill ease, out of malice and hatred, out of coldness and indifference, out of struggling and pushing. Out into fresh air and sunshine, life and living, fullness and plenty, joy and jubilation, wellness and wholesomeness, out into life, abundant life. All is well, all is well.

357

"It may be that I shall prove our friendship by asking you to wait in silence while I rest with you, assured of your Love and understanding. So wait, so love, so joy."

TWO LISTENERS

Rest. Rest in God's presence. Let go of all distractions. Switch off your phone or phones, switch off all radio, TV, music players and PCs. Sit still. Sit comfortably. Close your eyes and ask God to take all distractions away from you. Repeat a prayer, an affirmation or a mantra slowly. Concentrate on the words. If your mind wanders bring it back to the present. Listen to the sounds around you. Feel your body. What is pressing in on your skin and where? Breathe in and out, in and out. Know that God is with you. God loves you. You are surrounded by love, God's love. You are bathed in a cocoon of light and warmth. Peace descends slowly like the dripping of water, drop by drop. Second by second, moment by moment you are being filled with light, love, warmth and peace.

God is with you. God is with you. All is well. All is well.

"Am I not meek?
I give my hand, my lips, my cheek,
My dear, to you,
My life, my soul; and shall not rue.

MAX EHRMANN

Surrender. We all surrender to something. We surrender to our addictions. We surrender to food, to drink, to lust, to work, to more, more, more, to an ideal, to changing the world, to changing others or to a sexual relationship. What are the ruling passions of your life? We surrender to our ways of thinking, to our core beliefs. Why do you get out of bed in the morning? Do you live for yourself, your children, your marriage, your sport, your job / career, your country? Do you live for the next cigarette, the next drink, the next sexual experience, the next pill or the next fix? What are the ruling passions of your life? What can you not get through the day without? Are these things addictive and compulsive or life-enhancing and positive?

The positive things have no compulsion about them, just a gentle discipline and awareness that they are good to do. God's hand is very gentle. He gently and slowly herds us in the direction that is good for us and our total well-being. The world of addiction and craziness clamours loudly. The Lord's hand is gentle and the Lord's voice is soft and persistent. Listen to the still small voice, yield to the gently guiding hand. All is well. All is well.

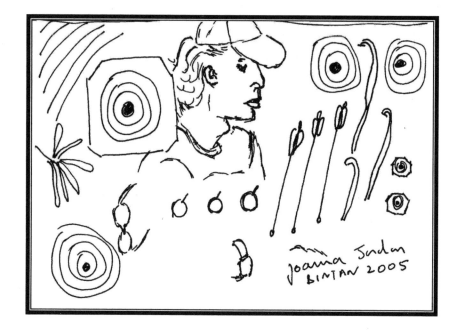

"HERTOG"

WEEK 46

"Dazed and confused by the changes which have taken place, they are not sure what they want."

RICHARD WEIGHT

"The upright shall praise your name, the honest dwell in your presence."

PSALMS 140:13

Who are the "upright"? They are those who are upstanding, those who stand up, stand up for what is right. They are those who stand firm. To be upright is to have dignity, clarity and poise. The upright are not bowed down with guilt or shame or woundedness. They are well. They are strong. They are doing what is right for them. They are acting according to their own truth and wisdom.

To be upright, to be truly upright you need God's help and the best way to get it is to talk to him. The best way to talk to God is to praise him. Praise opens the door to grace. Praise opens the door of communication to God. It clears out resentment and fear, jealousy and fear. When you praise God you focus on the existing good. This opens the door to present good and the future good.

To be honest first with yourself is essential for growth and change. No clarity will come to you unless you are honest with yourself. You cannot be honest with others until you know yourself and see yourself and the situation you are in clearly. You must first see before you can communicate it to others.

To dwell in God's presence is a marvellous thing. Every moment you spend in God's presence is wonderful.

"The 'War on Terror', should not be a war on Afghanistan or Iraq or North Korea or Syria or Iran or whatever place we'll end up invading. It should be a war on our own dark impulses."
MICHAEL MOORE

Murderous impulses comes from within. The ability to obey someone else's command to kill comes from a deadened self, a spirit that has been taken over by others, a conscience that is stifled. No fully alive, alert human being could deliberately kill another person. To be fully alive is to be fully human. When you have felt your own humanity fully you can recognise another person's humanity. Once you see another as a human being like yourself, you cannot deliberately kill that person.

In order to kill another human being, the killer must dehumanize his or her victim. An abortionist can only perform an abortion if he or she views the baby to be killed as an embryo, a foetus, the contents of the womb, or the pregnancy. No abortionist could do what they are doing if they were completely aware of the baby's life, of the baby's humanity and the baby's natural desire to live, to grow and to come to birth.
Solders kill 'targets' or 'the enemy' or inflict 'collateral damage' on the civilian population. They do not view themselves as killing people.

We all need to look at our own impulses. Do not deaden your conscience. Look to yourself and your past actions and inactions squarely. We are also responsible for what we did not do. If we ignore the plight of another human being we are responsible for this neglect, for the effect of our non-intervention.

"God saw all he had made, and indeed it was very good."
GENESIS 1:31

Value your life. Your life is precious. It is precious to you. It is a gift from God. It is the only life you know you definitely have. Some believe in reincarnation. I do not. It may or may not be true. Whatever is the truth of it, your life now is real. You are definitely alive now and able to take in the contents of this book. Your life is also precious to other people. You may or may not know who they are. But everybody who has contact with you even by sight, is affected by you, sometimes positively and sometimes negatively. You may live alone and have very little contact with other people, but your presence is felt by other people around you.

You have great power and potential. At this present moment, you have the power to open your heart to the whole universe, to love everyone and every being created in it. Open your heart a little, bless everyone you met or have had contact with today. Today is a good day. No day is lost if one loving thought comes into your head. No day is lost if the smallest of insights come into your mind about yourself or others. No day is lost if you do the smallest of kindness for someone. All is well. All is well.

"We have only a short time to care for those to whom we are bound by ties of love. Do not hesitate. Seize the moment."

ROBERT L BELL

Who are we "bound by ties of love" to? Everyone, not just the people we are related to by blood, by duty or by sexual contact. Everyone includes all we meet or have contact with during our day; all who cross our path. They are put there for a reason. The reason is love, to love yourself and to love them. Loving them could mean saying no to any unacceptable behaviour. That is, any behaviour that transgresses your dignity as a human being. Loving them could mean accepting all obvious goodness from them to as a gift from God. Loving them could mean accepting all obvious badness from them as their's alone and leave it with them, do not take it on board. You love yourself by learning the lesson that person has to teach you. You can learn quietness from the talkative, gratitude from the ungrateful, love of self from the abusive and the self-centered, to love from those who pour out hatred, self-worth from those who treat you with contempt, self-protection from the aggressive and the predator. Everyone has something to teach us. Learn your lesson quickly and it will not have to be repeated.

I have eight children with the Lord. This book is dedicated to them. Their names are Ann, Margaret, Beatrice, Sarah Rachael, Mary and Michael, Deirdre and finally Dermot. These are all children that I miscarried early in their lives. Sarah Rachael is the twin sister of Marion, my only living daughter. Mary and Michael are also twins.

Several years after the last baby died in early miscarriage, I was going through a period of grieving for them. This time I was stuck in the grief. I asked my daughter Marion (then about nine years old), to pray for me before I went to bed this night. Around 5.00 a.m. I woke to go to the bathroom and returned to my bed. I slept upstairs and my younger children slept downstairs. There was a wooden uncarpeted staircase in the house. Just as I was drifting off to sleep again, I heard the pat-pat of bare little feet on the stairs. As I lay in bed, my back was towards the bedroom door, I heard the child open the door and felt him get into bed behind me. I thought I had better turn over and see who this was. When I turned over there was nobody there. Into my mind flooded the consciousness that this was Dermot, the last miscarried baby. I could see him in my mind's eye at the age he would have been had he lived. He communicated to me that he and his brother and sisters were all well, that I need not grieve for them any more, that they were all happy, that they were with me and would all pray for me all the days of my life. He also communicated to me that I would be a great success.

The next day I woke up and all the grief had gone; it never came back.

I want to tell you the story of the big red apple. One day I was going on a journey with three of my children. The car I was driving was old and the radiator was leaking. I had a small amount of money with which to buy food. The journey was such that it would mean being out for two meals. For some reason I had no food with me. Along the road the radiator steamed up. So I pulled into the side of the road. There was a wide grass verge on this road. I stopped the car and got out with a can of water to fill up the radiator. After I did that I straightened up and look around. There was an enormous red apple in the grass. It was the size of a turnip. I picked the apple up and brought it to the car. It was perfect. We all had a share of this apple. It filled the four of us up. That was our lunch.

On the journey back I gave a lift to a strange man going along the country roads we were travelling. The radiator boiled up again. This time I had run out of water. The strange man said "Do not worry, pull over here. I know where there is a stream nearby." It was pitch black out. He got out and came back with the can full of water. I sorted the radiator out and off we went again.

At the next town we pulled in. The man got out. I saw a chip shop. There I was able to get a very large portion of sausages and chips for the money I had with me. For the price of one portion the chip man gave enough for four.

"JEAN MARIE"

WEEK 47

"But they will not be solved at all unless people see them as both outrageous and solvable, just as slavery was felt to be by twelve men who gathered together in James Phillips's printing shop in George Yard on May 22, 1787."

ADAM HOCHSCHILD

I would like to tell you the story of the expanding petrol. Once I was on holiday in France with four of my children. Everything had cost much more than expected and I was left with a small amount of money on the last day.

I had to drive to the car ferry. On the map it looked like a journey of 100km and I had enough money for petrol to do that journey. I bought the petrol and set off. After a while I realised that my estimate was wrong and that the journey was closer to 150km. I started to worry about petrol as I had no French money and no plastic cards either. My son Oliver, who was navigating us, was sitting in the front seat. On all the previous journeys in France he looked out for the signs and gave me directions. He fell asleep. I saw a sign for the next town that we were to bypass and turned off the road we were on. After 100m, I realised that I had come off the main road. I continued on, as I was afraid to use the petrol needed to do a U-turn and return. My son slept away. I watched the petrol guage and started to pray that I would get to the ferry. Once there, I knew I would be all right. I had Irish money to buy petrol once I got to the other side. I kept on the road. We passed through some amazing landscape and directly through some small French villages. We passed a sign for St Michael's church. I keep watching the petrol guage. Suddenly it started to rise. It went up one notch then two notches then three. After about 20km we rejoined the main road. We arrived safely at the ferry port.

Afterwards I was able to look up a map and found that the road I had taken cut 30km off the journey.

"In the conflict between Nature and your brain, back Nature; if you fight her, she will eventually destroy you. The secret therefore is to improve on Nature in harmony with Nature."

ANTHONY DE MELLO

Man has been given stewardship over this earth, not ownership. We are responsible for how we take care of ourselves, our families, our country and the earth itself. We are the dominant species on this earth. With that comes responsibility and accountability. We are all responsible for our own actions and inactions.

An owner can do what he or she likes with their property, but a steward is answerable to the owner for the care he or she takes of the property. We are answerable to God the Creator of heaven and earth for the care we take of the planet. We are also answerable for the care we take of our own bodies and the bodies of those who are put into our care. We arose out of nature. Nature is the blueprint for our existence. First there was the earth and the sky, then the sea and the sky, then the plants and the animals; we arrived last. All other systems were put in place before us. It is very daring of God the Creator to create beings in his own likeness and give them free will. No other beings have free will in the manner that we have it. We can freely choose to create or destroy, to maintain or dismantle. The choice is ours. God will always help you make good choices, choices for your higher good and other's. Ask him, ask him now.

"To be in the state called love you must be sensitive to the uniqueness and beauty of every single thing and person around you."

ANTHONY DE MELLO

We are conditioned, in the west, to think of love in terms of sexual relationships and mainly exclusive sexual relationships. To have an exclusive sexual relationship with someone is a decision. You decide to have sexual relations with that one person only. It is a good decision. It cuts down on sexually transmitted diseases and leaves the door open for children to enter into a stable household. Exclusivity is a decision and a commitment however long it may last.

There is confusion between love and sexual commitment. There is confusion between feeling love and loving. True love is awareness and acceptance. To accept someone completely as they are is true love. The commitment in love is to be true to yourself. When you are true to yourself and accept yourself as you really are then, you can accept others for what they are and maintain your dignity and personal integrity.

When you accept yourself absolutely and unconditionally then you can accept life absolutely and unconditionally. Then you see beauty all around you. Love flows out from you to all around you and back again. Love much. Love always. Love yourself.

"The child, like the innocent animal surrenders to its nature to be and becomes quite simply what it is."

ANTHONY DE MELLO

As adults, we have lost this innocence. The way back is full of pain. We need to let go of so much learning and conditioning. Rigorous self-honesty is needed; constant standing back and observing what we are doing and how we are reacting. In order to be free to be what we were meant to be, we must first see what we are now, what we have become. So much learning is unlearning. So much growth is letting go; letting go of attachments, letting go of compulsions, letting go of addictions, letting go of false beliefs, letting go of bad lessons learned. Be your best self and grow where you are planted. Today you are in the right place for you. Look around. Everyone you meet today is sent to teach you. Everything that happens today is for your benefit. All is well. All is very well.

"Power is just God in action. Therefore whenever a servant of mine, however weak he humanly may be, allows God to work through him, then all he does is powerful."

TWO LISTENERS

The book this quotation is taken from was written in 1932 by two English women. Both had known poverty, tragedy and loss in their lives. They believed that God spoke directly to them when they prayed together and they wrote down what he said. They chose to remain anonymous and called themselves 'Two Listeners'.

It is not always easy to see God in action within or through yourself. It is easier for other people to see things happening through you. The more you surrender your will and your life to God, the more God can use you for good. You not only need to surrender your will but also to act on any promptings you get.

One Sunday, many years ago, I decided to visit a beauty spot in west Cork. On the way I called into a woman I had met while working in the area. She had told me she was living a lonely and isolated life there and wanted to move but could not get anyone to buy her house. I called in and she agreed to come with me and my children to the lake. Before I called she has reached a point of deep despair. She had lain down on her bed to die. I did not know that, but something had prompted me to go and visit her. I called in some months later when I was in the area and she had a buyer for the house. The next time I passed the house was sold and the new owners installed.

If you get a prompting, obey it. You may not know why you are doing it but God does. He needs hands and feet to do his work.

"Is the Lord's rejection final?
Will he never show favour again?

PSALMS 77:7

The writer was in the depths of despair when he wrote this. He felt God had abandoned him. He felt utterly rejected and dejected. But it did not last long. Soon he remembered the times God had helped him. He remembered the good things in his life, all the battles fought and won, all his personal victories, all the doors that suddenly opened, all the traps that he had avoided. He knew then that God was with him in the past, was with him in the present and would be with him for evermore.

It is not always possible to feel God's presence. It is wonderful when you do, but the feeling passes. God is present in our lives whether we feel him or not. We often need to be reminded of all he has done for us in the past and trust and believe he is doing it in the present, and that he will be there for us in the future. God does not change. We do. God does not turn away from us. We turn away from him. All is well. All is well.

"DISAPPOINTMENT"

WEEK 48

"A reproof makes more impression on a person of understanding
than a hundred strokes on a fool."

PROVERBS 17:10

"Right in the nuclear family…, a resident crazy maker may often be found pitting family members against family member, undercutting anyone's agenda but his or her own."

JULIA CAMERON

Unless you are very clear and focused on your own life path, others can constantly knock you off. There are a lot of "crazy makers" or energy vampires in the world. They feed off other people's energies. In their lives it's their will be done and to hell with everyone else's. More than that, they use everyone else around them to achieve their own ends. They are expert at manipulation and distraction. They are brilliant at deflecting their blame and guilt on to others and getting them to absorb it. They themselves are then able to operate without guilt or taking responsibility for their actions. They have an uncanny ability to pick people who will easily take on guilt that is not their's to bear.

Be alert. Stand back. If you are reacting strongly to someone, ask yourself what is really going on here? Why are you reacting in such a way? If you really want to see the truth of what is happening to you it will become clear in time. You will always be shown your own truth. So keep the focus on yourself. In a strange way, whatever situation you are in today you have chosen it. The closer you get to God, the clearer you see yourself, the better your vision of yourself will become and the better your choices will be. The healthier your visions become the better your life will be.

"Creativity lives in paradox: serious art is born from serious play."

JULIA CAMERON

Play is so important. We all need play. Young children do it automatically. Only severely traumatized children will not play. Play brings us into the present. Play takes all heaviness of spirit away from us. Play opens us up to joy and love. Play brings our imagination up front. Play often. Play with yourself. Play with children. Play with other adults. Buy yourself some toys. What toys did you want as a child but were deprived of? Go out and buy some now or something similar. Balls of every shape and size are good. Blowing bubbles is good, great fun. So are hula hoops. Dolls and teddy bears are very emotional. Buy whatever you want, whatever you did not get as a child or did not get enough of. Buy a kite and have a go at flying it. Is there any sporting activity, creative activity or performing art you wanted to do as a child but could not do? Now as an adult you can do it. So take action, book your own dance lessons, music lesions, art classes, riding lessons or sailing lessons. Whatever you wanted but did not get, give to yourself. Be your own good parent. Give yourself what you needed then and still need now. Have fun. Today is the day. Start living today and everyday. Have fun, lots and lots of fun.

"In the middle of difficulty lies opportunity."
                                    ALBERT EINSTEIN

All difficulties are sent to challenge us. It is not just the challenge of the difficulty itself. It is the fact of the difficulty. If it is something that keeps recurring, then you need to look at the pattern and what is causing it. If the difficulty is a car that has broken down yet another time, you have to decide if you want to fix it again or scrap it. If you fix it, do you use it or sell it on? Once you have dealt with the immediate difficulty the question is why has this been happening? It could be that you would be better off without a car. You could use walking, cycling and public transport to get you about. It could be that a consciousness of lack has you in a situation where you cannot afford a decent car to fulfill your transport needs. It could also be that you are unconsciously stopping yourself from going forward. Maybe you do not want to go where you are heading.
There are always challenges in life. There is always something to learn. Sometimes we are presented with the means to learn the same lesson again and again until we get it.
        In my dreams cars symbolize freedom. Strangely enough, at the present point in my life I am car-less and I feel freer than I have ever felt in my adult life.
All is well. All is well.

"Mel lived with his aunt, who acted as his housekeeper, but 'slanderous tongues spread serious accusations against them.'"

KATHLEEN JONES

Malicious gossip is so destructive. It spreads suspicion, fear, ill will, blame and shame. It undermines the person that spreads it and the person it is aimed at. It is a subtle enemy working in the dark. Like a bad odour it spreads about the place affecting all in its path. Trying to defend yourself against unfounded and false accusations is a waste of time. The truth is your only shield. Do not entertain any thoughts of what 'they' are saying. The truth is the truth and in time it will become apparent to all. Pray for all who speak ill of you. Pray for them and send them love. This malice has nothing to do with you. Keep on praying for them and they will either disappear out of your life or change their attitude and behaviour towards you. The more malice that comes in your direction the more you need to pray for the people concerned.

All is well. All is well.

"The ship's Captain was surly, and did not want to take him as a passenger, though he had money for his passage. We are not told how a runaway slave acquired it. However, when he turned away, disheartened, some of the crew called him back."

KATHLEEN JONES

This is about St Patrick when he was a young man and had escaped captivity and was trying to get back to Britian. Patrick accepted the answer of the captain and turned away. It was then that the miracle occurred and a change of heart came to the crew. Acceptance comes first before change. First we need to accept where we are before we can move on. We need to accept the fact of a situation first, totally accept it before any change can come about. It could be that no change is needed or that the change we thought was needed is not the one that is really needed. Sometimes there is just nothing we can do for now. It is not the right time for change. Maybe now is the time for recuperating and building up strength. Now is the time to relax and let God take care of the problem. Now is the time to enjoy yourself and have some fun. Maybe now is the time to surrender the whole problem and its working out to God.

"There are no outsiders here."

RICHARD MOHAN

This is a quote from the leaflet of instructions to pilgrims to Lough Derg. Lough Derg is an island in the middle of a lake in Ireland. It is a place of pilgrimage and penance. As a pilgrim you fast and go around in your bare feet. When your feet are bare, you are very exposed. In a way your whole body is exposed to the elements. If the ground is wet, the wetness soaks into your body through the soles of your feet and up into your core. This also happens with the cold and the feel of the stones. Your feet contain the nerve endings of your whole body. A lot of people have ugly, misshapen feet, toes and toenails, and calluses, welts, fungal infections, blisters and rough skin can all be exposed to view. Your bare feet sense everything. They sense the vibrations from the earth and the feel of the stones. When everyone is vulnerable together it makes you feel tender towards each other. Jealousy, hatred, envy, spite and malice often come from a perception that others have it better then us. They have more possessions, more ease, more respect and more status.

When a group of people are all vulnerable together and united in a common purpose, it produces a feeling of fellowship. The greater the vulnerability the greater the fellowship.

"WILD LIFE"

WEEK 49

"A fool takes no pleasure in understanding
but only in airing an opinion."

PROVERBS 18:2

"Grant to me that I may be made beautiful in my soul within, and that all external possessions be in harmony with my inner man."

SOCRATES

I think that all our "external possessions" are always in harmony with your inner self. If our home is in a mess then we are in a mess. If our possessions are full of clutter then our minds are full of clutter. So if you want to clear your head, clear out your attic, your tool box, your sewing box, your personal papers or your sock drawer. If we are living in a dark and depressing place, then there is darkness and a sense of lack in our consciousness. Open the windows. Let in the light. Find another place to live. Change your external environment and your inner life will change too. Change your inner life and your external life will change too, in time. The external and the internal influence each other. Decide what you want in your life. If you want love send out love to other people.

If you want to be wealthy surround yourself with things that make you feel rich. Maybe a piece of velvet or silk, a china cup and saucer, a good pen, a leather bound book, a gold ring, a dish of strawberries and cream, Earl Grey tea or a cloth handkerchief. Anything that will make you feel rich and privileged. There is a time for feasting and a time for fasting. There is great abundance in this life. It is God's will for us that we should be provided for, in all that we need and more.

"I am in the world only for the purpose of composing."
FRANZ SCHUBERT

How wonderful it is that Schubert knew the purpose of his existence. How great it is to have a clear idea of your special purpose in life, the work that is for you alone to do. Not everybody has such a clear vision of their life. Sometimes life goes in phases. There could be a different purpose for each phase of life. I think we are always called to learn and to grow, not just in our bodies but in our minds, hearts and spirits.

Ill ease points to some imbalance in our lives. There is something that is not right. It could be lack of acceptance. First we need to be fully aware of how things are before we can accept them. Then only when we have fully accepted them can we progress to action. Action will then bring about change. Is there anything we have a hankering to do? Anything we have always wanted to do but did not? Anything you have seen yourself do in your mind's eye but never even tried to do? Well make a list of all those things. Look at this list and start doing them one by one. Soon you might just find the thing that is the special purpose of your life, your special talent.

"Grant me contrition of heart so that I may not be in disgrace; O Lord, protect me and grant me tears."

                                        CELTIC PRAYER

"Grant me tears." Tears are healthy, tears are healing, tears release pent-up emotional pain. Tears are the balm for the wounds of the heart. Without tears there can be no real healing. Tears open the way for the healing balm to pour into our hearts. Tears wash away all resentment. Tears heal the heart of all woundedness. Tears release tension, transforming energies. Tears soften the heart. When we open ourselves to tears, we are vulnerable, human and open to receiving love. Without tears there is no emotional growth, no true change. At the heart of tears there is absolute truth and the love of God, pulsating, powerful, triumphant true love. Tears can only come when you yield, when you stop fighting and surrender. When you are crying you are vulnerable and open. You need God's strong arms around you before you can cry in complete safety. Rest, rest, rest and know that all is well.

"They will have their meal now, and will not go hungry."
ST BRENDAN

Supply, God will supply all our needs in perfect time, in his own way and in great abundance. In as great abundance as you will accept, as you will allow or as you can imagine.

In nature there are both times of feasting and times of famine, great abundance and withdrawal of supply. Constant abundance is not good for us. After being showered with abundance, sometimes the supply is withdrawn for a time. Too much abundance leads to gluttony and laziness. It could also lead to us believing we are all-powerful. True power is in God's hands. We need to know that and appreciate it.

A time of fasting from any or all kinds of excess is beneficial. We may be indulging in excessive amounts of food, drink, sensual delights, company, leisure, money, material possessions and all forms of self-indulgent passions from which a total fast or temporary fast is necessary. We may impose a fast on ourselves or it may be imposed on us. Either way, doing without certain things or people is good for us. When we regain them again, gratitude comes naturally and so does appreciation. God works miracles both directly and through other people. God is both the giver and the gift.

"Don't row so hard, or you will exhaust yourselves. Is almighty God not the helmsman and captain of your ship? Do not strain yourselves, since he guides us where he will."

ST BRENDAN

This is so difficult. It is so much easier to strain and push and force things to be the way you want them to be, or else to turn away completely by ignoring the existence of the situation, thereby opting out of all responsibility for it. The middle ground is much more challenging; to do what you can do and let God take care of the rest.

"Is almighty God not the helmsman and captain of your ship?" Sometimes I let him and sometimes I do not. Life is definitely easier when I stop straining and trying to force solutions, especially solutions that involve other people's responses. It is easer to let God show me the way, to let God take over the helm. It is easer to stop the 'white knuckling' and let God guide me, let him take over. Sometimes I need to let go completely first, then, start again under God's guidance, allowing him to gently guide me though the situation. I need his constant help to keep me on the path once started. I am so prone to distraction. I need his help to gently bring me back on course every time I wander off. All is well. All is well. All is well.

"Every human being has a sort of dignity or wholeness in him, and out of that develops relationships to human beings, tensions, misunderstandings, tenderness, coming in contact, touching and being touched."

INGMAR BERGMAN

Yes, we are all unique, absolutely unique, no matter how similar we are, even identical twins have a uniqueness, an absolute separateness that makes them different from each other and everyone else. This makes life, our life very precious. Life is a gift to the individual. All of us, all of us have a unique spirit which reflects our Creator, our will, our circumstances, our experiences, our interactions with others and our inheritances. We all have a genetic, a cultural and a spiritual inheritance. Our genetic inheritance comes from our natural father and mother. We inherit the culture of the country we are reared in. Our spiritual inheritance comes from our family tree. We are affected by the sins of and on our forefathers and foremothers back seven generations. On the positive side all our ancestors who have passed into the fullness of life are there for us praying for us and our well-being. The negative effects from our family tree can be neutralized by prayer and fasting. Unless they are neutralized in our lifetime the effects will be passed to the next generation.

Because we are unique, relationships with other people can be difficult, very difficult sometimes. We need other people to help us in practical matters, to reassure us, to validate us, to enlighten us, to make us laugh, to help us cry and always, always to teach us valuable lessons about ourselves, our existence and indeed the existence of God our Creator.

"MOTOR BIKES"

WEEK 50

"When you are down and out,
People just pass you by.
Yes, I see spirits in the sky."

CHRISTY MEEHAN

"Moreover, I have God as my authority, he who knows all things even before they happen – that he frequently warned me, a poor ignorant orphan, through divine revelations."

ST PATRICK

God does warn us. For me I perceive it in my gut as a strong tightening or a physical revulsion. If something is wrong for me to do I feel it in my gut. Any time I ignored it and went ahead with whatever I had planned anyway, I suffered for it. Things did not work out and I had a hard time getting myself out of the mess I got into. We have free will. God has given us free will. He does not stop us doing anything. We have the privilege to choose our actions. But God will guide us, if we ask him, and let us know which way is the best way forward for now and which way is not good for us now. A certain way may be bad for us now but good for us at another time. There is a right time for everything.

There was a time I was in a crisis and a lot of people were advising me to take a certain course of action. It seemed wrong to me. Another suggestion was made. I did that one. Afterwards I had peace, all hysteria and panic left. I did not know why but all fear left me. It was not until several years later that I realised that the action I took at that time protected myself and my children from great harm. At the time I did not have the knowledge to choose that option knowing the full consequences of it, but God did and he communicated it to me. Keep an open mind and a listening ear. Listen to the still, small voice. It is always there, guiding you in the right direction.

"Many animal stories were told about Kevin: there was the otter which swam to the shore every day with a fish in its mouth for the monks, until one monk tried to trap it for its pelt and it swam away never to return."

KATHLEEN JONES

This is a reference to St Kevin of Glendalough. When the monks were fully dedicated to keeping contact with God, their needs were provided for. The otter was acting in complete accordance with the will of God. The monk who decided to trap the otter had become greedy and the blessing was withdrawn.

I was once in a holy place where it was believed that Mary the mother of Jesus, was appearing to a group of young people, every day at 6.00 p.m. I was outside the church one evening at 6.00 p.m. There were some tall trees there, with hundreds of noisy birds. Precisely at 6.00 p.m. all the birds stopped twittering completely. It was if a conductor in the sky said "Shhh", and the birds obeyed instantly. After the apparition finished, the birds gradually, started up squawking again. This really impressed me. Who can control the birds of the air? No human being can, only the Creator.

"This is the land which you have sought for so long, you were not able to find it immediately because God wished to show you his many wonders in the Great Ocean."

ST BRENDAN

St Brendan lived in Ireland in the sixth century. He founded a monastery in Clonfert. The story of his voyages were written down in the tenth century. During his seven year voyage on the Atlantic Ocean he is believed to have reached America. There is no proof of this at this time.

We all have our voyages to make and we all have our promised land. God is truly the helmsman of our ship of life. He will bring us to our promised land when conditions are right. We have to be right. We have to be ready.

We reach adulthood with a mixed bag of good and bad, positive and negative thinking, woundedness and wholeness. We are now totally responsible for our lives and well-being. Now with God's help we can release all the buried pain, retrain our thinking and heal our wounded hearts. This is our journey, our journey towards health, healing, wholeness and well-being, true self-love and love of others.

Bon voyage.

"She was caught in heavy rain and returned soaked to the skin. Finding little gaps, the sun shone into the house. Her eyes deceived her and mistaking the suns rays for a solid beam of wood, she hung her wet clothes on it... the clothes did remain hanging on the delicate sunbeam."

COGITOSUS

Cogitosus wrote this story of St Bridget, an Irish Christian woman living in the fifth century. Miracles were common according to the stories of the time. However many modern scholars discount these stories as they were not written down until centuries later.

Miracles do happen once you are in God's care. During times of financial lack, money has appeared in my purse. Money has also appeared on my path ready for me to pick up. Once a large amount appeared in my bank account. I had not put it there. One Christmas I had no money for food. I went down the road to the local church to pray. When I came back home there was a brown envelope stuck in the back door. It contained money sufficient for my needs but no note. To this day I have no idea who put that money there. The more I trust that God will provide, the more he does. Once I thought it best to do nothing and God would do everything. Well that did not last long! Today I know that I need to do my bit and God will do the rest. I will do what I can and God will do what I can not.

"The emotions may be endless. The more we express them, the more we may have to express.

E M FORSTER

Emotions are powerful feelings. They bring with them tremendous energy. This energy needs to go somewhere. There is a healthy place and an unhealthy place for this energy. Sadness needs to be released in tears and lamentations. True sadness is due to loss. Loss of life, loss of safety, loss of property, loss of love, loss of dreams, loss of expectations, loss of dignity, loss of abilities and loss of health. All losses need to be mourned. If they are not mourned at the time of the loss, the sorrow is put on hold. The memory with its energy is stored in the body where it eats away at your vitality and health. It takes a lot more energy to suppress unexpressed emotions. This is energy you could use for living and living well.

Anger is another emotion which brings with it a lot of energy. True anger is a reaction to a transgression on your dignity as a human being. This transgression could be against someone you are responsible for or a group you are aligned with. True anger is powerful as it engenders an explosion of energy to take immediate action in a situation. If this energy is buried, then it can spew out in all directions hurting people who have nothing to do with the original transgression.

Fear in its original healthy form is there to warn us of danger and to release energy to be used for fight or flight. Healthy fear is to be used on the spot. Prolonged fear or reactive, buried fear inhibits action and thought. In reactive fear the true source of the fear is gone. Something in the present is triggering an old fear. If you are afraid today what is causing it? Are you in danger? If so, do something about it. If not, trace the fear back to its source.

"She dresses herself to keep him with her, but it's no use – after a month or two, the wonder of a woman wears off."

SEAN O'CASEY

"The wonder of a woman wears off." All new pleasures wear off. The effect of any kind of indulgence wears off quickly. If you are seeking the thrill of the effect of pleasure, it will wear off quickly. Then you will want more, and the second time the pleasure will be less delicious. As you seek more and more the thrill gets less and less. Then you can get hooked into a cycle of depravity. The thing that gave you pleasure initially now becomes your God. You keep turning and turning to that thing for effect. It could be sex, or drugs, or alcohol, or food, or power, or money, or work, or status, or relationships. Whatever it is, it is a false God and it needs to be deposed.

First you must recognise it for what it is, a false God that is leading you down a path of destruction. Any thing that you cannot do without for a day or a number of days, which is not necessary for survival, is an addiction, a false God. A false God offers empty promises. What is the payoff for sticking with the person or thing you are addicted to? If you are willing to let go of whatever it is you are addicted to, then the help that you need to do so will come. The day will come when you will be free and enter your promised land of plenty.

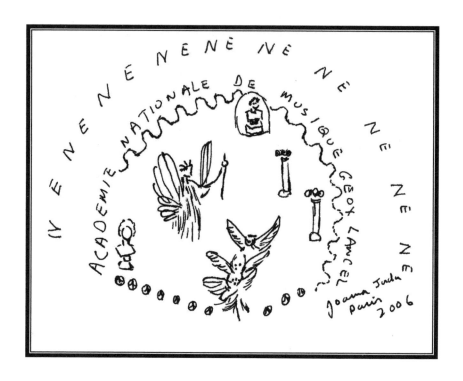

"THE OPERA HOUSE"

WEEK 51

"In the beginning God created heaven and earth."

GENESIS 1:1

"The problem with needy people is that they can't take in anything around them."

SUSAN JEFFERS

I was once walking down a street in a former Eastern bloc country. I noticed that the street was deserted. I looked around and saw a line of riot police walking alongside us. I told my friend. She had not noticed. I noticed, and was ready to run if necessary. That taught me how valuable awareness was. It can be a matter of life and death. So, be alert. Look around you. What do you see? What can you hear? How does your body feel? Are you in any physical pain? Are you in emotional pain? Let that go for now. How is your eyesight? Do you need glasses? Are the ones you are using good enough? Is your mind going around in circles? Stop. Stop all compulsive, obsessive thinking. Come into the present. Feel your body. Is there anything pressing into you? Where? Are you uncomfortable in any way? Release the discomfort. Be in your body completely. You have a good body. It was given to you to use well. Ask forgiveness for all the times you abused or mistreated your body. All the times you put toxic substances into it. All the times you used it in a sexually inappropriate way. All the times you overworked it or under-exercised it. All the times you exposed your skin to strong sun, heat or cold. All the times you did not take good care of yourself. Ask your body to forgive you. Ask God to forgive you. Make a commitment to treat your body well from now on.

"My Peace. Never a Peace that is a truce with the power or evil. Never harmony it that means your life music being adapted to the mood and music of the world."

TWO LISTENERS

"Your life music." What is your life music? I think it is your true self, your divine self-expression, your uniqueness, your true inner self. How many of us are dancing to our own life music?

The "world" here, I think means other people and what is currently socially acceptable among the people we live with. Fashions change not just in clothes, homes, furniture and cars but also in ideas. At one time it was believed that to spare the rod was to spoil the child. Now, in some countries where that belief was held, it is a criminal offence to slap a child. Our perception of good parenting changes from generation to generation and from culture to culture.

If you align your will with God's will for you, then you will know what is the right course of action to take. This can often conflict with the current acceptable norm. The "world", does not like people to deviate from the norm, to do their own thinking. Living your own truth can bring conflict. You can not control other people's reactions to your behaviour. You can only control yourself. If other people do not like what you are or what you do or say, there is nothing you can do about it, except pray for them. If you continue to pray for them, then ill will, will fade away and the truth will emerge in time.

"When there is no one or nothing that has your attention the orchestra will play a music of its own."

ANTHONY DE MELLO

The "orchestra", referred to here is your own life music. It is the well-spring of life within you. When you have let go of all obsessions and addictions, of all destructive attachments to ideas or to people or to substances, then your own soul music begins to play. Life becomes easy, you know if you are being sucked into destructive situations or relationships and you just do not go there. Even it you visit for a while, you do not take up residence there. You experience a new freedom. You make good decisions quickly. You have the freedom to enjoy all the wonder and beauty in the world. You see the roses and avoid the thorns. You are grateful for all that you have. Ill will vanishes from your consciousness. Love flows out freely from you and freely back to you. You are alive. All is well. All is exceedingly well.

"The word discernment comes from distinguishing, therefore, since in us it distinguishes between good and evil, the mediocre and the perfect."

ST COLUMBANUS

St.Columbanus was an Irish saint and a founder of monasteries. Here he is referring to the working of the Holy Spirit within us.

Every day you need to discern between good and evil in your impulses, in your actions and in your motivations. Every day you need to make good decisions. Some people prefer a life of slavery, where someone else makes all the decisions, to a life of freedom, where they themselves make most of their decisions for their daily life.

Freedom can be very frightening, as freedom brings with it responsibility: the responsibility to live well, to use time, money and resources well; the responsibility to take good care or yourself; in fact, the complete responsibility for your total well-being. When you take full responsibility for yourself, you can not blame anyone else for the state you are in. That is a huge challenge. Today you are alive. You have survived until today. Congratulations, you are a success. Today is the first day of the rest of your life. Live well. Enjoy all the good there is in today.

"There is a logic of colors, and it is with this alone, and not with the logic of the brain, that the painter should conform."

PAUL CEZANNE

Paintings that appeal to us and that generations upon generations of people respond to, are calling us to something deeper than the logic of our brains. They are appealing to instinct, to our innate sense of right and wrong and you do not contact this by applying brain logic. Brain logic is necessary, and a part of life. It helps us to construct buildings, make useful objects, plan and organise our practical lives both individually and collectively. It is necessary, but it is not the only logic in existence. Some things are just perfect and there is no explaining it. There is a feeling of rightness. It is conforming to other laws. It is tapping into other realities. The creative person is a channel between another realm and their particular medium, be it paint, words, sculpture, music or any other form. The creative person needs to open themselves up to this power and allow it to flow in. Let go of all distractions and let the creative, life-affirming power flow in. Harness it and use it for good. Enjoy. Enjoy. Have fun, innocent child-like fun. Have plenty of it.

"The quality of life is in proportion, always, to the capacity for delight. The capacity for delight is a gift of paying attention."

JULIA CAMERION

Pay attention. Pay attention to what is going on around you. Stop reading on public transport, look at the people around you. Look out the window. What do you see? What do you smell? What do you hear? Look at the sky. What colour or colours do you see there? Are there any clouds in the sky? What shape are they? How do you feel in your body now? Is there any pain anywhere? Are you comfortable? Stop reading. Look around. What do you see? Life is full of wonder. Nature is the most wonderful creation. Nature is ever changing, ever complex, never boring; it has infinite variety. Are any two people exactly the same? No. Even identical twins are different in their spirits and in many small ways. Wake up. Be alert. Pay attention. Life is for living. Life is going on all around you. Even in a prison cell there could be a family of spiders. Look, observe, pay attention.

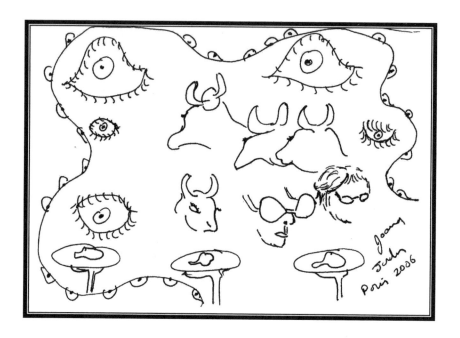

"THE COWS"

WEEK 52

"The Grace of our Lord Jesus Christ be with you all. Amen."

REVELATION 22:21

"No man even for his body's sake can afford to indulge in hatred. It is like repeated doses of poison. When you are urged to get rid of fear, you are not listening to a moon-struck idealist; rather you are hearing counsel that is as significant for health as advice about diet."

ALBERT EDWARD DAY D. D.

Fear and hatred generate poisons within your body. These are real not imaginary. Your body reflects the long-term effects of your soul. All negativity builds up in your body and affects your health. Every illness, every bodily dysfunction, has its cause in mental and spiritual ill health. If your body is ill today, take care of the physical first. Do whatever you can to relieve your sufferings today. Then look to the spiritual and the mental. By taking care of the physical first you are paying attention to your body and taking care of it.

The cause of your condition is deeper. The illness itself will give you a clue. Your back supports your body and its internal organs. If you are having back problems ask yourself what area of life do I feel unsupported in? Could it be financially, or possibly in relationships? If you have problems with your circulatory system relates to you feelings and passions. What are your strong passions? If your blood is over-heated are you full of anger? You know the answers. God will show you the answer. He will show you the cause and what you need to do to release it. If it is a hereditary disease, then you may need to work on the clearing of your family tree. The answer is there and God is there to help you to freedom.

"Cease trying to forgive those who fretted or wronged you. It is a mistake to think about it. Aim at killing the self now – in your daily life, and then, and not until then, you will find there is nothing that even remembers injury, because the one injured, is dead."

TWO LISTENERS

I think the "self", referred to here is self-will or what some people call the ego. When someone injures you, do not take offence, let it go. If you need to protect yourself from further assaults then do so. When you take offence it is your self-will that is damaged. Let it go. It is not personal. Let it go. Bless the other person. Bless the situation. If you surrender your life and your will to God, then everything that happens to you is for your benefit or someone else's. All is for the benefit of the kingdom of God. Accept whatever happens and if action is needed then take it. First accept what happens. You may not know why it happened, but accept the fact of it. Know that God is working in there somewhere and it has the potential for great good to come out of it somehow. Let go completely of all occasions where you were wronged or felt wronged. Let it go. Pray for all concerned. When it comes into your mind, pray for the people concerned. Eventually it will go and you will be free.

"Compare the serene and simple splendor of a rose in bloom with the tensions and restlessness of your life. The rose has a gift that you lack: it is perfectly content to be itself."

ANTHONY DE MELLO

This sounds so wonderful: to be "perfectly content to be itself." Oh, how much unlearning do you need to do in order to accept yourself perfectly as you are? You need freedom from shame and guilt by facing squarely the things you are guilty of and those you feel guilty for but are not responsible for. The more you accept yourself as you are the more you accept other people as they are. Perhaps it would be best to start with what you do accept about yourself. Make a list. You can start with: I am alive.

Contentment and acceptance are very close. If you can accept yourself for what you are completely today, warts and all, you will be content. Just say to yourself or aloud: "I accept myself fully and completely as I am today." Repeat this over and over again. All is well.

"Several of Nature's People
I know, and they know me –
I feel for them a transport
Of cordiality - "

EMILY DICKINSON

Emily Dickinson spent most of her adult life living the life of a recluse. She lived at home with her family. She rarely left the house and garden. She spent a lot of time in her garden growing fruit, vegetables and herbs for the home. She did preserving and cooking and wrote poetry. Sometimes she wrote her poetry on the back of recipes. She did not believe in waste.

To be alive is a gift, a gift from God. A unique gift granted to you. Look around you. There is wonder and beauty to be found. Look well. All of nature reflects God's hand. Look and you shall find. What can you see? Look with wonder at all before you. Children are beautiful and precious and wonderful. Are there any children about? The younger a child is the closer they are to their Creator. Some believe that our spirits exist before our conception, that our spirits had been looking and waiting for the perfect match of parents to bring us to into being. This is hard to believe, as parents always fall short of perfection.

Whatever the truth is, we are now alive and life is a gift. Spend it well. Today is the only day that you know for definite that you have to live. Use it well. Miracles of change can happen at any time. Miracles of existence are present all the time. Look for them.

"On one occasion her foster mother was seriously ill. She was sent with another girl to the home of a certain man called Baethchu, to ask for a drink of ale for the sick woman. They got nothing from him.... They came to a certain well where she filled three containers. The liquid was tasty and intoxicating and her foster mother was healed immediately."

ST BRIGID

This is a wonderful story. Many such miraculous events are recorded in the annals of the early Irish saints. A lot of the stories were handed down by word of mouth and written down centuries later. Historians disregard them as there is no proof. I believe that a lot of these things did happen because firstly there were so many of these and similar stories and secondly because I have experienced some small, miraculous events in my own life.

One day I was without any money and I needed to buy some food for myself and my children. I was sorting through some old papers in a box and came across a book I had not seen for some years. I opened the book and there were some notes, £31 exactly. I was delighted. At the time it was enough to feed the family for the most of a week! It was the exact amount of money that was taken from me, some years previously, in very painful circumstances. The date on the money was the same year that the money had been taken from me. I had opened that book several times in the interveaning years and there was no money there.

414

"But you delight in sincerity of heart, and in secret you teach me wisdom."

PSALMS 51:6

"In secret you teach me wisdom." God teaches us all secretly, privately. All our insights, all our moments of clarity, come to us secretly in the deepest recesses of our hearts. God leads us gently by the hand to the right book, the right person, the right talk, the right film, the right incident, for us to learn what we need to know next. In the deep recesses of our hearts all is known. In the deep recesses of our hearts God lives. His guidance is gentle, very gentle. We need to listen very carefully for his word. Sometimes we need help to find our way there. Once there we need no one else.

The year has come to an end. What have you gained from this gift of another year? Have you learned anything? Have you come closer to God your Creator? Have you received love and given love? Have you looked at your life and its problems squarely in the eye? Have you admitted to yourself and another person your wrong-doings and weaknesses? Have you made amends for your wrong-doings and non-doings? Are there some things you omitted to do this year? What are they? Make a list. Start on the first thing on the list in the New Year and work your way through. Have you taken time for fun and play this year? What is the most enjoyable thing you did this year? Do more of it next year. Have you laughed at yourself, danced in the rain or serenaded your beloved? If not do it next year.

My final quotation is from the booklet "The Father speaks to his children". It is believed to be part of a message given to Mother Eugenia by God the Father in 1932.

"Realise then, O men, that for all eternity I have but one desire, to make myself known to men and be loved by them. I wish to stay forever with them."

THE FATHER

PEN AND INK DRAWINGS

WEEK	LOCATION	DRAWN	TITLE
1.	Sherkin Island	Ireland	"Trap"
2.	Cork City	Ireland	"Shandon"
3.	Cork City	Ireland	"Life"
4.	Dublin	Ireland	"Kate"
5.	Blarney	Ireland	"James and Tomas"
6.	Co. Cork	Ireland	"Waterfall"
7.	San Giovanni Rotondo	Italy	"Wilting"
8.	Mount Mellery	Ireland	"The Abbot"
9.	Cork City	Ireland	"Man Smoking"
10.	Blarney	Ireland	"Pre -historic"
11.	Blarney	Ireland	"Jazz 11"
12.	Blarney	Ireland	"Jazz 111"
13.	Cork City	Ireland	"South Mall"
14.	Cork City	Ireland	"Fitzgerald Park"

417

15.	Ballincollig	Ireland	"Seat"
16.	Gougane Barra	Ireland	"Toilet"
17.	Blarney	Ireland	"Blarney Castle"
18.	Co. Cork	Ireland	"Harbour View"
19.	Brisbane	Australia	"Lamp"
20.	Aran Island	Ireland	"Wall"
21.	Grand	Canary Island	"Ships"
22.	Grand	Canary Island	"Harbour"
23.	Budapest	Hungary	"Jewish Cemetery"
24.	Budapest	Hungary	"Veritas et Vita"
25.	Budapest	Hungary	"Feet"
26.	Budapest	Hungary	"Swan"
27.	London	England	"Birds of a Feather"
28.	London	England	"Restaurant"

29.	London	England	"The Eye"
30.	London	England	"Pots of Money"
31.	London	England	"Watching Me, Watching You"
32.	London	England	"Browns"
33.	London	England	"Covent Garden"
34.	London	England	"Haven Descends"
35.	London	England	"Pelicans"
36.	London	England	"D"
37.	London	England	"Reflections"
38.	London	England	"City Guardians"
39.	Cookham	England	"Alethea"
40.	London	England	"Arab Woman"
41.	London	England	"Lamp in Park"
42.	Bintan Island	Indonesia	"Trapeze"

PEN AND INK DRAWINGS CONTINUED

43.	Bintan Island	Indonesia	"Flowers"
44.	Bintan Island	Indonesia	"Orchid"
45.	Bintan Island	Indonesia	"Hertog"
46.	Bintan Island	Indonesia	"Jean Marie"
47.	Paris	France	"Disappointment"
48.	Paris	France	"Wild Life"
49.	Paris	France	"Motor Bikes"
50.	Paris	France	"The Opera House"
51.	Paris	France	"The Cows"
52.	Gougane Barra	Ireland	"Swans"

INDEX

A

ABANDONMENT.............Nov. 24
ABUNDANCE..................Jan. 2, March 7, May 25, Aug. 7,
                                   Nov 17, Nov. 19
ACCEPTANCE................July 3, July 16, July 30, Sept. 20,
                                   Oct 15, Nov. 30
ACTION........................Aug. 11, Sept. 12, Sept 18
ADDICTION...................July 25
ALCOHOLISM................March 1
ALERTNESS...................July 20
ANGER..........................April 28, Oct. 3
ANGLES........................June 27
APPRECIATION.............July 6
AUDACITY....................Aug. 15
ATHORITY....................May 30
AWARENESS.................May 15, July 27, Aug 6, Sept.13,
                                   Oct 9, Dec. 22

B

BEAUTY........................May 8, July 6
BEING...........................Jan. 30
BETRAYAL....................Oct. 30
BLESSINGS...................April 20, May 12, Sept. 6
BLOCKS........................June 22
BOLDNESS....................Sept. 26

C

CENTEREDNESS.............Aug. 13
CHALLENGES................Jan. 4, Jan 27, Jan. 29, May 19,
                                   Nov. 28
CHANGE........................Jan. 11, Feb. 8, July 19
CHILDREN....................Jan. 18, Feb. 17, June 27, Aug 22,
                                   Oct. 30
CLARITY......................Jan. 3, Sept. 27, Oct 13
CLINGING.....................July 28, Aug. 2
COMMUNICATION..........Sept. 11

CONSCIENCE.................March 27, Aug 2
CONTENTMENT..............Dec 26
CONTROL.....................Oct. 1
CORE BELIEFS................July 23, Aug. 4, Nov. 7
COURAGE.....................March 6, March 9, May 29,
                          July 5, Sept. 26, Oct. 12
CRAZYMAKERS..............Nov. 26
CREATIVITY..................Aug. 18, Aug. 23, Sept. 17,
                          Nov. 27
CRITICISM....................Aug. 21
CURSES........................May 12

D
DARKFORCES...............Jan 9
DARKNESS....................April 18, Sept. 24, Oct. 17
DEATH.........................March 5, March 31
DELIGHT......................Dec. 22
DESTINY......................June 6
DISAPPOINTMENT..........Aug. 10
DISCERNMENT...............Dec. 20
DISCIPLINE...................May 18
DIVINE RIGHT................June 5
DREAMS.......................Sept. 5
DUTY...........................May 10

E
EMOTIONS....................Dec. 14
EVIL...........................Jan. 6, April 19, May 1, June 14,
                          June 30, Aug 1, Oct 17
EXTERNAL
POSSESSIONS.................Dec. 3

F

FAITH.............................Jan. 6, Feb 7, March 3

FALSE GOD'S...................Jan. 22

FANTASY........................June 4

FEAR.............................Feb. 13, March 12, March 13, May 31,
July 31, Aug 8

FORGIVENESS.................Feb 19, May 11

FREEDOM........................July 21, Oct. 4, Oct. 23, Nov. 8

FULFILMENT....................Sept. 5

G

GIVING...........................April 11, May 5, June 18

GOD IN ACTION...............Nov. 23

GOD'S LOVE....................Jan. 16, Jan. 20

GOD'S PRESENCE.............Aug.28

GOD'S SPIRIT..................Jan. 13

GOD'S WILL.....................Feb. 6, Feb. 27, April 27, May 9,
June 5,
Dec. 18

GOD WITHIN...................March 2, April 17

GOOD NEWS...................March 15

GRACE...........................Aug. 30, Dec. 31

GRATITUDE....................Jan. 25, Jan 29, March 14,
March 17, April 23, June 29

GRIEF............................Jan. 19, June 8, June 14, Nov. 16

GROWTH........................Feb. 26, March 19, May 16, Aug.
3, Oct. 2

GOSSIP..........................Nov. 29

GUIDANCE.....................Jan. 31, April 19, Sept. 14,
Dec. 7

GUILT............................Oct. 26

H

HAPPINESS.....................Jan 17, July 17, July 24

HARMONY......................April 27, Oct 27, Oct 31,
Nov. 3,Dec. 1, Dec. 3

HATRED.........................Dec. 24

HEALING......................June 21, Sept. 4

I
ILL – WILL.....................Oct. 20
INNATE........................Dec. 21
INNOCENCE..................Nov. 22

J
JOY.............................May 3, May 8, June 8, June 9,
                             June 11,
                             Sept. 3, Sept. 28
JUDGEMENT..................April 30
JUSTIFICATION...............Oct. 19

K
KILLING.......................Feb. 16, April 19, Nov 13
KINDNESS....................Feb. 1, June 13, June 21
KNOWLEDGE................March 22, March 28

L
LAUGHTER...................Feb. 2, July 5
LEARNING....................Aug. 25
LETTING GO..................Aug. 22
LISTENING...................March 16
LOSS..........................June 23, July 6
LOVE..........................Feb. 15, Feb. 28, March 23,
                             April 5, April 16,
                             June 16, June 23, June 26, Oct 5,
                             Oct 24, Nov. 2, Nov 15, Nov 21
M
MEDITATION................Oct. 22, Nov. 9
MIRACLES....................Oct. 16, Dec. 13, Dec. 28
MISTAKES...................Aug. 9
MONEY.......................Jan. 1, Jan. 23, July 7, Oct. 18

N
NATURE......................June 19, July 14, July 18,
                             Aug 18,Nov 20

NEEDS.........................Feb. 9
NEIGHBORS..................March 30

O
OPPORTUNITY...............March 30

P
PAIN............................June 11, June 15, July 25,
                              July 30, July 31,
                              Aug. 3, Oct. 10
PEACE..........................June 20, July 3
PLAY............................Aug. 16
PLEASURE.....................Dec. 15
POWER.........................Feb. 3
PRAISE.........................March 17, May 7
PRAYER.......................May 21, June 11, June 12,
                              June 30, July 11,
                              Oct. 8
PRECIOUS.....................Nov. 14
PROGRESS.....................June 28
PROTECTION.................March 21, April 24, May 2,
                              May 4, May 26,
                              June 30, July 10, Oct. 8
PROVIDANCE................Nov. 17, Nov. 19

R
RAGE...........................Feb. 22
REALITY.......................July 13, July 16, Sept. 1, Nov. 6
RECEIVING....................Jan. 1, Feb. 14
REGRETS.......................May 16
RELATIONSHIPS.............May 23
RESENTMENT................April 4, Dec 24
REST............................June 2
RETRIBUTION...............March 10
REVELATION................Sept. 25
RISK TAKING.................Aug. 31, Sept. 18, Oct. 6
ROUTINE......................March 26

S

SARCRIFICE....................Aug. 27

SELF EXPRESSION............March 7, March 29, May 14, Dec. 4

SELF LOVE.....................Jan. 15, Jan. 24

SELF RESPECT.................Aug. 29

SELF WILL.....................Nov. 1, Dec. 25

SERVICE.......................April 7

SEX............................March 20, Nov. 5, Nov. 21

SHAME........................Aug. 20

SIMPLICITY...................April 3, May 28, July 9

SIN............................March 8, June 14, June 25, July 21

SORROW.......................June 12

SOUL MUSIC..................Dec. 19

SPIRITUAL BATTLE........Aug. 24

SUPPLY.......................Dec. 6, Dec. 11

SURRENDER.................May 9, May 26, June 13, June 23, Sept. 15, Nov. 10

STANDING STILL............Feb. 5, June 1, June 2

STILL CENTER...............Jan 8, Feb. 12

STRENGTH...................Jan 28, April 12, May 9, June 27

T

TEARS..........................Dec. 5

TEMPTATION..................June 1, July 2

THE PRESENT.................Feb. 20

THINKING.....................April 5, Oct. 29

TIME...........................Jan. 5, March 16, April 10, April 16

TODAY........................Jan. 10, March 24, May 24, Aug. 17

TOUCH........................Sept. 22, Sept. 29, Nov. 5

TRUST.........................April 25, May 22, May 26

TRUTH........................April 21, June 7, Sept. 19, Oct. 25, Nov 6

U
UNDERSTANDING..........Jan. 3, Feb. 21
UNIQUENESS.................Feb. 23, April 9, Sept. 21, Dec.8
UPRIGHT.....................June 12, July 26, July 28

W
WAITING.....................Feb.10
WANTING....................July 12, July 26, July 28
WARNING....................Dec. 10
WEAKNESS...................June 15
WELLBEING.................Sept. 10
WHOLENESS................Dec. 12
WISDOM......................Feb. 24, April 2, Sept. 8, Oct. 11,
                          Dec. 29
WISHES........................April 13, May 17, June 6
WOUNDS.....................Sept 7
WONDER.....................Dec. 27
WORDS........................Jan. 12

427

SOURCES OF DAILY QUOTATIONS

Al-anon and Alateen members. AS WE UNDERSTOOD.
New York: Al-anon Family Group Headquarters,
Inc. 1985

Allender, Dan. THE WOUNDED HEART. New York:
Navpress Publishing Group.1990

Anonymous. A CURRENCY OF HOPE. U.S.A.: Debtors
Anonymous.1999

Appleyard, Bryan. THE SUNDAY TIMES – CULTURE.
August 2005

Browne, Cathal. THE ADVENTURES OF PUCK. Galway:
Ainnir Publishing. 2001

Brown, Dan. DIGITAL FOTRESS. New York: Thomas Dunne
Books.2004

Cameron, Julia. THE ARTIST'S WAY. London: Pan Books.
Macmillan Publishers Ltd. 1995

Curtis, Susan & Fraser, Romy & Kohler, Irene. NEAL'S
YARD NATURAL REMEDIES. London: Arkana.
1988

De Mello, Anthony. THE WAY TO LOVE. New York:
Doubleday.1992

Dostoyevsky, Fyodor. THE IDIOT. London: Penguin Books.
1997

Doyle, Roddy. THE VAN. Minerva Ed. 1993

Ehrmann, Max. THE DESIDERATA OF LOVE. New York:
Crown Publishers, Inc. 1995

Field, Lynda. 60 WAYS TO FEEL AMAZING. Shaftesbury
Element Books Ltd.1998

Gibran, Kahlil. LIFE'S WISDOM. London: Arrow Books. 2000

Gillman, Harvey. A LIGHT THAT IS SHINING. London:
Quaker Home Service.1997

Graham, John. WILLIAM PENN.

Grisham, John. THE BRETHREN. New York: Doubleday.
2000

Groening, Matt. BART SIMPSON'S GUIDE TO LIFE.
London: Harper Collins. 2000

Jeffers, Susan. FEEL THE FEAR AND DO IT ANYWAY. London: Arrow Books. 1991

Jones, Kathleen. WHO ARE THE CELTIC SAINTS? Norwich: Canterbury Press. 2002

Julian of Norwich. REVELATIONS OF DIVINE LOVE. London: Penguin.1998

James, Kelly. POEMS. Galway: Self Published. 2003

Kidd, Sue Monk. THE SECRET LIFE OF BEES.

Kraus, Nicola. Mc Laughlin, Emma. THE NANNY DIARIES. U.S.A. St. Martin's Press. 2002

Larsen, Earnie & Larsen Hegarty, Carol. DAYS OF HEALING DAYS OF JOY. Minnesota: Hazelton.1992

Lewis, C.S. THE FOUR LOVES. London: Fount. 1963

Moore, Michael. DUDE WHERE'S MY COUNTRY. London: Allen Lane. 2003

O'Casey, Sean. THE PLOUGH AND THE STARS. London: Macmillan. 1994

O'Connor, Frank. MY OEDIPUS COMPLEX & OTHER STORIES.
Harmondsworth: Hamish Hamilton. 1957

Padre Pio of Pietrelcina. LETTERS 1. San Giovanni Rotund: 1984

Rilke, Rainer Maria. LETTER TO A YOUNG POET. Norton. 1934.

Rinder, Walter. FOREVER US. Celestial arts. 1981

Roman, Sanaya. & Duare, Packer. CREATING MONEY. Ti Buron, CA: H. J. Kramer. 1988

Salinger, J. D. THE CATCHER IN THE RYE. London: Penguin Books. 1958

Scovel-Shinn, Florence. THE GAME OF LIFE AND HOW TO PLAY IT. London. Vermilion. 2005

Scovel-Shinn, Florence. THE SECRET DOOR TO SUCCESS. The C.W. Daniel Company Ltd. 2004

Shakespeare, William. HAMLET. London: Penguin. 1994

The Father. THE FATHER SPEAKES TO HIS CHILDREN. Italy: Associazione Dio e Padre – Casa Pater. 1982

The People of Ireland. BUNREACHT NA hEIREANN. Constitutuon of Ireland. Dublin: Government Publications.1937

Tolstoy, Leo. WAR AND PEACE. Ware: Wordsworth Ed.'s Ltd.1993

Truss, Lynne. EATS, SHOOTS & LEAVES. London: Profile Books Ltd. 2003

Two Listeners. GOD CALLING. London: Arthur James Ltd. 1991

Unknown. THE NEW JERUSALEM BIBLE. London: Dalton, Longman & Todd. 1990

Unknown. QUAKER TESTIMONIES. London: Quaker Home Service. 1988

Wright, James. A BLESSING in POETRY NOW. Dublin: The Celtic Press.1999

ADDITIONAL SOURCES OF WEEKLY QUOTATIONS

Adie, Kate. THE KINDNESS OF STRANGERS. London:
Headline Book Publishing. 2002

Bitel, M. Lisa. TALES OF SEX AND GENDER FORM
EARLY IRELAND. New York: Cornell University
Press. 1996

Dostoyevsky, Fyodor. CRIME AND PUNISHMENT. London:
Penguin Books. 1997

Hochschild, Adam. BURY THE CHAINS. London: Macmillan.
2005

Holm, Richard. AN AMERICAN AGENT. London:
St. Ermin's Press. 2005

Klare, Michael. BLOOD AND OIL. London: Penguin Books.
2005

Kowalska, Sr. Maria Faustina. A LITTLE BOOK OF SAINT
FAUSTINA. Dublin: The Columba Press 2005

Kowalska, Sr. Maria Faustina. DIVINE MERCY IN MY SOUL
– DIARY. Stockbridge, Mass.1987

Mezrich, Ben. UGLY AMERICANS. London: William
Heinemann Ltd. 2005

O'Farrell, John. I BLAME THE SCAPEGOATS. London:
Black Swan 2004

Paver, Michelle. FEVER HILL. London: Bantam Press, 2004.

Richardson, Cheryl. TAKE TIME FOR YOUR LIFE.
London: Bantam Books. 2000

Sherry, Norman. THE LIFE OF GRAHAM GREEN VOL.2.
London: Jonathan Cape. 1994

Studwell, Joe. CHINA DREAM. London: Profile Books. 2002

Weight, Richard. PATRIOTS. London: Macmillan. 2002